Escaping Salem

New Narratives in American History

Series Editors
James West Davidson
Michael B. Stoff

ESCAPING SALEM

THE OTHER
WITCH HUNT OF 1692

RICHARD GODBEER

NEW YORK   OXFORD
OXFORD UNIVERSITY PRESS
2005

Oxford University Press

Oxford   New York
Auckland   Bangkok   Buenos Aires   Cape Town   Chennai
Dar es Salaam   Delhi   Hong Kong   Istanbul   Karachi   Kolkata
Kuala Lumpur   Madrid   Melbourne   Mexico City   Mumbai
Nairobi   São Paulo   Shanghai   Taipei   Tokyo   Toronto

Published by Oxford University Press, Inc.
198 Madison Avenue, New York, New York 10016
www.oup.com

Oxford is a registered trademark of Oxford University Press

Library of Congress Cataloging-in-Publication Data

Godbeer, Richard.
  Escaping Salem: the other witch hunt of 1692 / by Richard Godbeer.
    p. cm.—(New narratives in American history)
  Includes bibliographical references (p.).
  ISBN 0-19-516129-7—ISBN 0-19-516130-0 (pbk.)
  1. Trials (Witchcraft)–Connecticut–Stamford–History–17th century.
    I. Title. II. Series.
  KFC3678.8.W5G66 2004
  133.4′3′097469–dc22   2004043399

Printing number: 9 8 7 6 5 4 3 2 1

Printed in the United States of America
on acid-free paper

for all those
falsely accused

CONTENTS

FOREWORD

IN MATTERS OF WITCHCRAFT, THE OUTBREAK AT SALEM VILLAGE is the Jupiter of the solar system. It has attracted more notice in the popular press—and even among scholars—than any other such episode in American history. Yet the sheer magnitude of the outbreak, with its multiple trials, attendant hysteria, and wide geographical spread, has created a kind of gravitational distortion that has colored our broader notions of witchcraft. Although Salem was not typical of most outbreaks in colonial New England, it remains, by default, the archetype through which most Americans understand, or misunderstand, the subject.

Yet Salem was not the only community to serve up a witch hunt in 1692. Farther south, another incident roiled the area around Stamford and Fairfield, Connecticut, without producing an equally lasting notoriety. As Richard Godbeer demonstrates in the engrossing narrative presented here, in many ways the Stamford controversy reveals more about the anguish and ambiguities of witchcraft than do the more frequently examined tumults at Salem. Godbeer has drawn upon a rich trove of court transcripts and depositions to recreate the events arising out of the fits of one Katherine Branch, a servant in the household of a respected Stamford townsman.

Escaping Salem is one of Oxford's New Narratives in American History, a series of books that foregoes the detached, often Olympian manner of much historical prose. We have challenged our authors to envision less traditional approaches to their subjects, both in method and in language. Godbeer conjures the world of Stamford in 1692 not by deploying the explicitly analytical techniques of the social scientist but through a deceptively simple rendering of events, viewed from the perspectives of the various participants. At the same time, the insights of the social sciences have not been neglected, for as the afterword reveals, they very much shape the way the narrative is drawn.

Readers may be surprised to learn that the men and women struggling to understand Katherine Branch's fits exhibited a broad range of emotions and ideas. They were not always eager to blame the Devil for Branch's afflictions, on the one hand, or to assume, on the other, that she was either an impostor or a woman beset by mental illness. In Godbeer's carefully reconstructed world, all these readings were options, as the natural and supernatural coexisted uneasily alongside folk wisdom, superstition, and skepticism, as well as the natural philosophies and theologies of early New Englanders.

James West Davidson
Michael B. Stoff
Series Editors

Acknowledgments

It was in the late 1980s that I first encountered the cast of characters whose ordeal in the year of their Lord 1692 this book reconstructs. The witch hunt that began in Stamford, Connecticut, a few months after the outbreak of afflictions in Salem Village appeared as a short case study in my doctoral dissertation and later in my first book. I had a feeling at the time that there was much more to be written about the Stamford witch hunt and its significance, but this was clearly another project for another day. Since then I have often used the transcripts in an undergraduate course that I teach on witchcraft in early New England. That experience has taught me that Stamford's witch hunt has much to tell us about the varied, often remarkably cautious, ways in which New Englanders reacted to allegations of witchcraft; it also shows with singular clarity how disagreements between neighbors over who or what was really causing an alleged bewitchment could compromise and undermine accusations. Above all, it is a gripping story that deserves to be told as such. Watching and listening as my students reacted to the documents, pondering the implications of their questions, and digesting their insights has been an indispensable part of the process through which the story of what happened that year took form in my mind's eye.

Now I have an opportunity to tell that story, thanks to Oxford University Press. Peter Coveney has my sincere thanks for shepherding this project so deftly over the past two years; working with Peter, his editorial assistant June Kim, production editor Celeste Alexander, and copyeditor Terri O'Prey has been a genuine pleasure.

I am also grateful to the John Hay Library at Brown University, the Connecticut State Library, and the Stamford Historical Society for preserving documents from the 1692 Connecticut trials and for giving me access to them. Local historians Ronald Marcus and Barbara Kaye have shared their deep knowledge of Stamford's past—I greatly appreciate their help and that of Irene Hahn, a volunteer archivist at the Stamford Historical Society. Many years ago John Demos kindly lent me his own painstaking transcript of the depositions from these trials; that transcription and David Hall's recently published edition of the trial documents, produced with the assistance of Emma Anderson and Anne Brown, have provided an invaluable basis for comparison as I developed my own version.

Writing has once again proven to be as much a collective as an individual endeavor that depends on the support and advice of friends and colleagues. Michael Bellesiles, Wendy Lucas Castro, Madeline Duntley, Mary Francis, Denise Garrison, Piotr Gorecki, and Elizabeth Reis offered insightful and encouraging comments on the manuscript at various stages of its development. Christine Heyrman, my professional fairy godmother who still casts her magical dust over all that I write, has been characteristically savvy and forthright in her exhortations. But my principal debt this time around is to Jim Davidson, who has guided this project from its first conception through to the final revisions of the manuscript. I have had more than my fair share of good fortune in teachers, especially in the craft of writing. Jim is my latest mentor. People who are almost always right can prove rather trying, but Jim somehow manages to be completely right and yet completely likeable—this is quite a coup. It has been a privilege and a pleasure to learn from so benign a master of the craft.

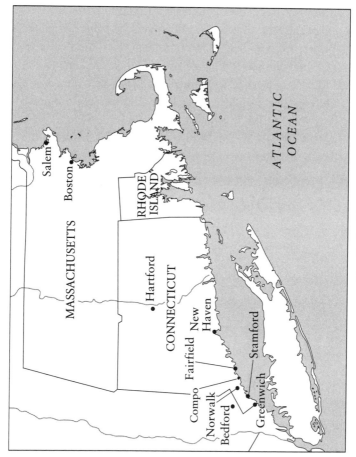

New England in 1692

PROLOGUE

"A Witch! A Witch!"

It was early one evening in June 1692 and dusk was falling over Stamford, Connecticut, a compact little town of some five hundred souls perched on the northern shore of the Long Island Sound. A young man named Ebenezer Bishop was strolling homeward through the town, hungry for his supper after helping one of his neighbors mend a broken fence. Mary Newman, a woman in her early thirties whom Ebenezer had known since childhood, was heading in the opposite direction. They greeted each other cordially as their paths crossed and Ebenezer continued on his way. But a few seconds later he came to an abrupt halt in front of Mister Wescot's house as a young woman's scream erupted from inside—a piercing, blood-chilling scream followed by a prolonged wail of pain and fright.

Ebenezer shuddered. He looked back over his shoulder, exchanged a meaningful glance with Mary, and then quickened his

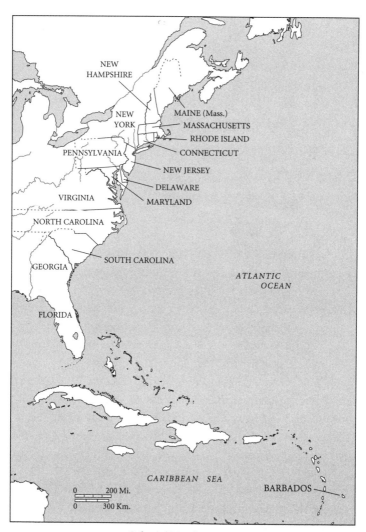

NEW
HAMPSHIRE

MAINE (Mass.)

NEW
YORK

MASSACHUSETTS

RHODE ISLAND

CONNECTICUT

PENNSYLVANIA

NEW JERSEY

DELAWARE

VIRGINIA

MARYLAND

NORTH CAROLINA

SOUTH CAROLINA

GEORGIA

FLORIDA

*ATLANTIC
OCEAN*

CARIBBEAN SEA

BARBADOS

0   200 Mi.

0   300 Km.

Colonial North America

pace to put some distance between him and Mister Wescot's house. The scream came as no surprise to him or Mary. Both had witnessed the horrors that tormented the Wescot household. Like many of their neighbors in the close-knit town, they had visited Daniel and Abigail Wescot to lend support as the couple kept watch over the afflicted young woman in their charge. What they saw there had convinced Ebenezer and Mary that Katherine Branch, a seventeen-year-old maidservant in the Wescot home, was bewitched.

Kate, as she was known, had been in that tormented state since the end of April. Without warning and for no apparent reason she would suddenly collapse into agonized convulsions, crying out that she was pinched and pricked by invisible creatures, weeping and moaning in helpless terror. At other times she would sink into a paralyzed trance, stiff as a board and completely senseless. She told her master and mistress that during these fits she saw cats that sometimes transformed into women before her eyes and then changed back into animal form. It was these creatures that attacked her, she said.

Stamford, the site of these ghastly afflictions, was a remote southwestern outpost of Puritan New England. Although much closer to New York than to Boston, its character and layout were typical of a New England town. First settled in 1641, Stamford had grown largely through natural increase. The town was remarkably uniform in its ethnic and spiritual makeup: residents were mostly of English descent and identified with the Puritan faith. Most of the houses were clustered together within easy reach of the meetinghouse, which enabled the faithful to keep close watch over each other, protecting their neighbors and themselves from sin. With few exceptions, the families who lived there supported themselves by farming on strips of land that surrounded the town. The townsfolk aspired to a life of peaceful order and purposeful spirituality. Yet Stamford was at the present time anything but peaceful or orderly. Indeed, it was under supernatural attack.

Though Ebenezer Bishop had never before witnessed such horrors, he knew well that afflictions of this sort did occur and that they were often the handiwork of spiteful neighbors who knew how to wield occult powers against their enemies. Many were the stories he had heard growing up of strange fits and other bizarre ailments, the unexplained death of livestock, the mysterious withering of crops, and the premature spoiling of food. To be sure, such incidents could sometimes be traced to natural causes. Yet Ebenezer knew that supernatural forces were constantly at work in the world. Sudden losses or mishaps might well be judgments from God, sent to chastise sinners and encourage moral reformation. But sometimes these misfortunes turned out to be the handiwork of someone closer to hand with much less exalted intentions, a malign neighbor using dark cunning to torment and even destroy—witchcraft might be to blame.

Daniel and Abigail Wescot had feared from the very onset of their servant's afflictions that Kate was under an evil hand. Still, they were willing to consider other explanations and so called in the local midwife to examine the young woman for signs of a physical ailment, which would be a much less disturbing explanation for her torments. The midwife was reassuring: she evidently thought that Kate's symptoms might well have a natural cause. But when the treatment she recommended had no lasting effect, the Wescots concluded that their servant's affliction must be supernatural. Kate herself was clearly convinced of that. "A Witch! A Witch!" she cried out in her fits. "Why will you kill me? Why will you torment me?"

Meanwhile, the Wescots' neighbors argued among themselves over the cause of Katherine Branch's fits. As news of her torments spread rapidly throughout Stamford, townsfolk went to observe the young woman's symptoms and to help the Wescots look after her. Some declared that Kate was clearly under an evil hand, but others suspected that she was counterfeiting her symptoms. It was after Ebenezer Bishop heard these conflicting reports that he decided to go and see the fits for himself. Those who gathered in the Wescots' home witnessed strange and disturbing occurrences: mysterious lights that entered and traveled through the house at night; the inexplicable appearance of bruises on Kate's body; the materialization of pins in her hand that Kate claimed were put there by witches; and, of course, the fits themselves. Kate's body went through horrifying contortions that seemed far from natural and she fought off those who tried to restrain her with a strength that she had never before exhibited. Though some townsfolk remained suspicious, many became convinced—among them Ebenezer Bishop—that Kate was indeed bewitched.

If so, the likely culprit was close at hand. Elizabeth Clawson, a longtime resident of Stamford, had quarreled often with the Wescots and many other townsfolk. Indeed, Goodwife Clawson was notorious for her argumentative nature and her vengeful spite. Some locals believed that she used occult powers to injure her enemies: confrontations with Goody Clawson were often followed by strange ailments or mishaps in the households of those with whom she quarreled. No one in the town was surprised when Katherine Branch named Elizabeth Clawson as one of her tormentors.

There were others. The Wescots had also quarreled with Mercy Disborough, who lived several miles away just outside the county town of Fairfield. Kate had never met Goodwife Disborough, but she had overheard conversations about her. Goody Disborough's neighbors had long suspected her of witchcraft and Kate now claimed that Mercy was afflicting her as revenge for the quarrel with her master and mistress. As the days and weeks passed, Kate named additional women as her tormentors. Some were Stamford residents; others Kate knew only by reputation . . . until they began to visit her as apparitions during her fits.

How many witches, wondered Ebenezer as he neared his home, were involved in tormenting Katherine Branch? Why had they combined forces to afflict this one maidservant? And how would the authorities deal with them? News had reached Stamford that almost two hundred miles to the north, just outside Boston in the village of Salem, a group of girls and young women were wracked by fits similar to Kate's. They also had accused witches of afflicting them. Information about the afflictions in Salem had arrived piecemeal: there were as yet no newspapers in the North American colonies and so news spread slowly up and down the Atlantic coastline, through letters or gossip carried by travelers; those who journeyed by land would stop at taverns along their way and share news with locals as they quenched their thirst. The road that connected Stamford to other towns was rocky and treacherous, with long and often ill-maintained bridges that stretched precariously over deep ravines. Yet the town was not cut off from the rest of New England: it had a fine natural harbor and most travelers journeyed to and from Stamford by water. According to the merchants and seamen who sailed into the harbor, carrying with them news of the outside world, dozens of Massachusetts residents had already been arrested and charged with witchcraft. Was that about to happen in Stamford?

The Salem witch hunt is without doubt among the most infamous events of American history. Indeed it has the dubious distinction of being one of the few occurrences from the colonial period with which most modern Americans are familiar. During 1692 over one hundred and fifty Massachusetts women and men were formally charged with the crime of witchcraft; many more were named informally as suspects. By the time that the trials came to a halt, nineteen of the accused had been hanged. Several others died in prison and one man was crushed to death during interrogation. This was by far the largest witch panic in colonial America: it convulsed an entire region and even today, over three hundred years later, it continues to fascinate and appall students of history.

But it was not the only witch hunt to occur in New England that year. The other took place in Fairfield County, Connecticut, and began with Katherine Branch's torments. That other witch hunt of 1692 took a very different course from the panic in Massachusetts. Stamford townsfolk were for the most part remarkably cautious in reacting to Kate's accusations. The officials responsible for handling Connecticut's witch crisis refused to make hasty judgments about the accused and insisted on weighing carefully the evidence against them: if witch suspects were to hang, their guilt must be irrefutable. *Escaping Salem* provides a corrective to the stereotype of early New Englanders as quick to accuse and condemn. That stereotype originates with Salem, which was, in its scale and intensity of hysteria, unlike other outbreaks of witch hunting in New England. Stamford's witch hunt was much more typical.

There were striking parallels between the Salem and Stamford witch panics. Both began with strange fits that many locals came to believe were caused by witchcraft. In both colonies accusations of witchcraft spread beyond the immediate community in which the afflicted lived. And there was no consensus in either Massachusetts or Connecticut as to whether the accused were guilty as charged. In the early summer of 1692 magistrates began convicting and hanging witch suspects in Salem based on evidence that some observers found problematic. Those who criticized the court's actions—a growing chorus of magistrates, ministers, and other "gentlemen" in and around Boston—did not doubt the reality of witchcraft. Most of them also believed that the afflicted in Salem Village were bewitched. But how, they asked, could a court of law be sure that particular suspects had committed what were, after all, invisible crimes? The evidence presented against the accused was, they argued, insufficient to convict. By October of 1692 attacks on the court had become so forceful that the governor of Massachusetts, also worried by news that his own wife had recently been named, felt he had no choice but to suspend the trials. There followed an agonized postmortem over what had happened and why. The Salem witch hunt has been notorious ever since.

The witch trials in Connecticut did not begin until September 1692. We know that those involved were aware of recent events in Salem and the increasingly controversial convictions. The magistrates presiding over the trials in Fairfield County were determined to avoid the fatal errors of judgment that they believed had occurred in Massachusetts. It helped the cause of restraint that there was only one afflicted person at the center of the Stamford panic and that her own trustworthiness became, as we will see, a subject of debate. In fact, the magistrates agreed to prosecute only those suspects against whom there was evidence from witnesses other than Katherine Branch herself. As a result, only two women came to trial: Elizabeth Clawson and Mercy Disborough. The limited scale of the witch hunt in Connecticut, especially when compared with what was happening in Massachusetts that same year, accounts for its subsequent obscurity. But for the two women on trial and those who accused them, Connecticut's 1692 witch panic was no trivial matter. What follows is the story of their ordeal.

That story has two phases. Initially, the witch hunt took the form of a local and informal crisis as Stamford residents came together to interpret Katherine Branch's fits. Neither the Wescots nor their neighbors assumed straight away that Kate's fits must be the result of witchcraft. These were by no means the blinkered and credulous New Englanders that persistent stereotypes might lead us to expect. Neighbors came to observe Kate partly out of curiosity, partly to support the Wescots, and partly out of genuine concern for the young woman. But they also wanted to test Kate's claims. The Wescots' home became a laboratory of sorts as the people of Stamford watched Kate closely and carried out experiments to ascertain whether her fits were natural, supernatural, or perhaps counterfeit. Once the Wescots and other townsfolk became convinced that witchcraft was causing Kate's afflictions, her tormentors had to be identified, evidence had to be gathered, and witnesses had to be willing to speak out. All of this was risky given that most previous witch trials in New England had not resulted in conviction—if witches were tried, acquitted, and released, they might wreak terrible revenge upon those who had testified against them.

The second phase of the story centers on the appointment of a special court to deal with the allegations against Elizabeth Clawson and Mercy Disborough. Both women were accused of having "in a preternatural way afflicted and done harm to the bodies and estates of sundry of their Majesties' subjects." Dozens of men and women now came together—as magistrates, jurymen, accusers, witnesses, and defendants—to participate in that most elusive of legal tasks, the prosecution of an occult crime. The two women had their supporters, especially Goody Clawson. But hostile witnesses related feuds and confrontations between neighbors, personal misfortunes that occurred soon after quarrels with the accused, and the venomous spite that apparently wove these stories together into a quilt of deadly vendetta. They had come to demand justice and retribution.

Yet the magistrates were committed to a careful and cautious sifting of that testimony, which placed them in potential conflict with those who believed that they and their neighbors had provided ample evidence to justify conviction. Much of the drama that unfolded in Fairfield County that year would center on the tension between fear of witchcraft and the scruples of the court.

Would the magistrates prove willing to convict the witches whom local residents believed to be lurking in their midst? If not, they might save two innocent women from the hangman's noose. Or they might fail the past, present, and future victims of witchcraft by freeing malign individuals who would then continue to wreak havoc in their communities. At stake were the lives of two women, Elizabeth Clawson and Mercy Disborough, as well as those of their alleged victims.

· One ·

KATHERINE BRANCH'S FITS

I‌T WAS A BEAUTIFUL AFTERNOON IN THE LAST WEEK OF APRIL 1692. Winter was giving way to a warm spring and the townsfolk of Stamford were once again released from cramped winter companionship. Most families lived in small timber-framed homes with only four rooms, two downstairs and two above. A large stone or brick chimney stood at the center of the house, at its base an open fireplace. The outside walls were covered with clapboard. Inside the house a narrow entrance hall divided the two rooms on the ground level. A stairway, usually built alongside the chimney, led to the upper chambers. The beams supporting the steep shingled roof remained exposed, as did the other woodwork—these were unpretentious, utilitarian structures. Windows were mostly small and the houses dimly lit even during the day. There was no storage space, other than wooden chests, and so clothes and other belongings were all on view amidst the bustle of domestic activity. Some families created more space by extending the rear roof and adding more rooms, but most Stamford homes offered little in the way of privacy and must have seemed especially crowded by the end of winter. No longer driven by the cold to huddle inside whenever they could, townsfolk now dispersed gladly into the fields, drawn by the freedom of being outdoors as much as the seasonal labors that came with springtime.

Abigail Wescot's husband, children, and servant had all left the house and she was enjoying a moment of peace. Though the Wescot family had not been spared its share of trials and tribulation, Providence now seemed to be smiling upon them. Her children were flourishing, even her eldest daughter Joanna, who some years ago had fallen prey to strange pains and frights but was now fully recovered. Abigail's husband Daniel, who at fortynine was her senior by just over a decade, had become a leading figure in the town. Daniel's prominence in local affairs had recently been confirmed by his election to a second term as one of Stamford's representatives to the colonial assembly. That their neighbors recognized Daniel's qualities was a source of much pleasure to Abigail. He was also a sergeant in the town militia and she hoped that he might one day become an officer. Meanwhile the Wescots' status in the town earned them the honorific titles of Mister and Mistress, much more satisfying than the modest though respectable prefixes Goodman and Goodwife. And besides, the linen was drying rapidly outside in the spring sunshine. Praise be to God!

The tranquil silence was suddenly shattered as Katherine Branch, the family's seventeen-year-old servant, burst through the door. She had been sent to pick herbs in a nearby field, but the wretched girl had none with her. Katherine was crying and moaning, her hands clutching her chest, and she was panting as though the Devil himself had chased her home.

"Well, where are the herbs?" her mistress asked sharply, resentful of this sudden end to her peaceful meditations. "What's the matter with you?"

Kate gave no answer, but fell to the floor, her hands clasped and her body strangely contorted; she wept piteously. Abigail's eyes narrowed. She neither liked nor trusted the young woman. Was this some trick to avoid completing her chores for the day? Or had something happened in the field to bring on this outburst?

A few hours later, Daniel Wescot returned home and Kate was still lying on the floor, her eyes red from crying and her hands clamped together as if held in place by some invisible force. He stopped short at the door, taken aback, and then shot a questioning glance at his wife. Abigail knew exactly what the flicker of panic in his eyes meant. He was recalling the torments that had assailed their daughter Joanna some years back. Daniel had never quite gotten over the horror of that ordeal. Their little girl had been plagued by spasms of pain and insisted that something or someone entered her room at night to torment her; she saw creatures running from one hiding place to another when no one else could see them. These disturbances continued night after night for three weeks. So frightened was the little girl that her parents could not persuade her to undress and go to bed in the house. Most nights they took her to stay with their neighbor next door, where she would calm down and eventually get some sleep. At the time Abigail and Daniel had worried that Joanna might be under an evil hand and so they sent her away to stay with friends in a nearby town. The torments subsided and Joanna returned a few months later.

Abigail understood why the sight of Kate contorted in fear on the floor would remind her husband of Joanna's affliction, yet their maidservant's condition was surely different. She had not said that anyone was after her. Indeed, she was refusing to say anything. She just lay there, weeping and whimpering. Best let her be, Abigail thought, and the episode would likely pass. If not, they could call in Sarah Bates, the local midwife. Daniel had often lamented that Stamford had no physician, but Abigail had faith in Sarah's medical knowledge and skill. Meanwhile they must try to remain calm.

Sarah Bates found Katherine Branch lying immobile on a bed. The Wescots, who were clearly anxious, told Goodwife Bates that their servant had taken ill the day before. Some of the time Kate lay rigid as if in a trance, but she also had screaming fits and at times cried uncontrollably. The girl had said little since the onset of these afflictions, though she did reveal during an interval of relief that whilst out in the field gathering herbs she had been seized with a pinching and pricking at her breast.

Goody Bates had no formal training as a medical practitioner, but she did have many years of experience in observing and treating her neighbors' ailments. Her expertise ranged far beyond midwifery. It was grounded in centuries of herbalist tradition as well as the shared wisdom of the local female community in which she was raised. The women of Stamford—young and old, mothers and daughters, household mistresses and their servants—gathered regularly to support each other as they braved the travails of childbirth and illness. Women like Sarah Bates emerged as experts from those communities of mutual care, their skills endorsed by the experience and gratitude of their neighbors rather than university degrees or formal apprenticeship. Goody Bates had a finely honed instinct for discerning what ailed a sick neighbor and was widely respected for her abilities.

Sarah understood that the operations of the human body could be disrupted by divine judgment and devilish intrusion as much as by natural ailment. Any responsible diagnosis had to take into account the possibility of supernatural intervention. God might have inflicted the symptoms as a punishment for sin; ideally this would prompt repentance and reformation as the inflicted person recalled the moral lapses that had provoked God's anger. She also knew of occasions on which experienced doctors and midwives had concluded that an ailing neighbor was bewitched. Katherine Branch's symptoms were certainly odd and resembled closely descriptions that Sarah had heard of bewitchment and demonic assault.

Kate's mother had also suffered from fits—the falling sickness, or epilepsy, as some called it. Perhaps Kate had a similar malady. But medical experts disagreed as to what caused the falling sickness: some argued that it was rooted in a natural disease, others that the symptoms were brought about in at least some cases by possession or witchcraft. Goody Bates saw no reason to ignore the possibility of a natural explanation. She advised the Wescots to burn feathers under Kate's nose, a method that she often found effective when dealing with fainting fits. The midwife then asked for a cup of water, drank gratefully, and exchanged a few pleasantries with Mister and Mistress Wescot. Before leaving she encouraged them to fetch her again if the servant's condition did not improve.

The following morning Mister Wescot came again for Goody Bates, this time, even more anxious. The feathers, he told her, had seemed to help at first, but Kate had since relapsed into a stupor: she was, he said, both senseless and speechless. Sarah found the servant much as Mister Wescot had described. Kate lay as though dead, her eyes half shut, though her pulse was beating normally. Mistress Wescot and her daughters were gathered round the young woman, watching closely.

Since the feathers had not produced any lasting effect, some other form of treatment must now be chosen. But what? Mistress Wescot wanted Kate bled. To be sure, purging the body of excess fluids so as to restore a healthy balance between the four humors—blood, phlegm, choler, and melancholy—could solve many physical disorders. Yet the midwife knew that bloodletting was risky when dealing with a patient who seemed so close to death. She said as much, but Mistress Wescot insisted that they try, so Goody Bates removed a pin from her pocket.

Just as she was about to prick Kate's foot, the servant broke out of her stupor and exclaimed, "I'll not be blooded!"

"Why?" asked Sarah, astonished that the maid should so suddenly revive.

"It would hurt me," Kate replied.

Mistress Wescot reassured her servant that "the hurt would be but small, like the prick of a pin." Kate then calmed down. Sarah observed the girl with growing suspicion as Kate held out her foot obligingly. This was a remarkably swift recovery from lying senseless on the bed. Sarah bled her a little and then Kate lay down again. A few minutes later, Kate suddenly grabbed the bedspread on which she lay and screamed.

"Mother," gasped one of the Wescots' daughters, "she cried out!"

"She is bewitched!" declared Mistress Wescot.

Sarah flinched, recalling that the Wescots had reacted the same way some years earlier when their daughter Joanna had fallen sick. But the midwife had no time to consider this before the servant girl surprised her again. Kate turned her head away from the Wescots as if she would hide it in the pillow—and then she laughed.

Goody Bates did not know what to think. Was Kate convinced that her sickness was natural and so surreptitiously laughing at her mistress for thinking that she was bewitched? Or was she faking her symptoms and enjoying her success in duping the Wescots? Or was the laugh itself a symptom of her fits? Determining the true cause of Kate's behavior was not going to be easy.

When Goody Bates had first voiced her opinion that Kate's affliction might well have a natural cause, Daniel Wescot was willing to entertain that possibility. After all, finding a natural explanation would spare them from having to confront the darker possibility that their household was once again under occult attack. But during the days that followed, all that Kate revealed of her strange afflictions made Mister Wescot more and more convinced that his servant was indeed bewitched.

Shortly after the midwife's second visit, Kate announced that during her fits she saw a cat that spoke to her. It invited her, she said, to go away to a place where there were "fine things" and "fine folks." There followed more fits and she seemed much tormented. When Daniel Wescot questioned her further, Kate said that the cats (for now there were several) told her they would kill her. A few days later she saw a room with a table on which was spread a variety of meats; there were ten cats eating at the table and they asked her to join them. But Kate told her master that she ran away to hide, explaining that she saw "a cat coming to her with a rat, to fling it in her face." Not long afterward she told him that the cats were again threatening to kill her, "because I told you of it." Sometimes, Kate declared, the cats turned into women and then back again, though who the women were she could not say.

One night, about two weeks after the afflictions had begun, Kate's fits became much worse and she suddenly cried out, "A witch! A witch!"

When her master asked what had happened, Kate said she had felt a hand reach out to her in the darkness.

As Daniel Wescot reflected upon Kate's fits, it seemed to him that the creatures she saw were more than likely witches in animal form, conspiring to lure his servant into their hellish band. He knew from the sermons he had heard on the subject that witches, the Devil's disciples on earth, were always campaigning to augment their hateful fellowship. It would not be surprising if they tried to tempt Kate with "fine things" and splendid feasts. Anyone could fall prey to such temptations—such was the moral weakness of all men and women. But Kate would be especially susceptible, given the circumstances under which she had come to live as a servant in his household.

It was not unusual for young people in New England communities to be "put out" by their parents to work in neighboring households so as to learn a trade or skill. Sometimes they lived there as well, especially if the distance between homes was great. Parents who feared that they were overly indulgent to their children might send their offspring to live for a while in households where they would receive a stricter form of governance: ensuring a proper sense of discipline and humility was much more important than the immediate comfort of children or their parents. Whether sent away to learn a particular craft or to be saved from the sin of pride, such children knew that their being put out was temporary; at some point they would either return to their parents or set up households of their own. But other young people went to work as servants because their families were unable to support them or because they had been orphaned. Such was the lot of Katherine Branch: her parents were dead. She had no inheritance to use as a dowry and so had little prospect of securing an advantageous marriage. Kate might well crave "fine things," ruminated her master, but she almost certainly would not get them. The servants of Satan were cunning: they knew the soft spots of potential recruits and went straight for them.

Any doubt in Daniel Wescot's mind that they were dealing with witchcraft disappeared once Stamford's minister became involved. The venerable John Bishop was an educated and experienced man of God: he had graduated from Oxford in 1632, just a few years after the first wave of Puritan settlers sailed to New England; he had served as pastor in Stamford for nearly fifty years. Mister Bishop visited the Wescots' home several times to observe and counsel their servant. On one occasion he brought with him Thomas Hanford, the pastor in nearby Norwalk since

1654. Both men were clearly convinced that Kate was bewitched. Surely they could be trusted to understand such things?

The Reverend Bishop explained to Kate that the witches wanted her to join them in secret devotion to Satan—hence their anger when she told her master and mistress about them. God preserve her from such assaults! Both ministers warned Kate that she must not yield or else her soul would be lost to the Enemy of mankind. On leaving the house, the two ministers promised to observe a day of fasting and prayer in company with the Reverend Abraham Pierson of Greenwich, a much younger pastor who had arrived in Connecticut the previous year. Daniel Wescot readily trusted their reading of the situation; he took comfort that they and the Reverend Pierson would be praying for his household in its affliction.

Before he left, John Bishop impressed upon the Wescots that they must keep a close watch over their young charge and be on hand at all times to protect her. Such was their duty as master and mistress. Like any other servant, Kate was a member of their family, albeit in a subordinate station. The Wescots were responsible not only for meeting her material needs—food, clothing, and shelter—but also for supervising her education and spiritual welfare. The Reverend Bishop taught in his sermons that the head of a family should think of himself as fulfilling the role of a priest within his household: he must do all he could to nurture the spiritual well-being of those living under his roof. A household mistress also had a crucial role to play, setting an example of Christian conduct and protecting the young people under her care from temptation. Given that Kate no longer had any parents of her own, the Wescots had a special responsibility to-

THE DEVIL AS A BLACK, HORNED CREATURE WITH WINGS, AC-COMPANYING WITCHES ON BROOMSTICKS *The woman on the ground may also be a witch, or the three figures on broomsticks may be urging her to join the witch confederacy. The crucial feature is the presence of the Devil—ministers insisted that he was behind all acts of witchcraft and that those afflicted by witches were in great peril since the servants of Satan often promised to end their torments if the victims agreed to become new recruits.* (SOURCE: WOODCUT FROM *WONDERS OF THE INVISIBLE WORLD*, AN ACCOUNT OF THE SALEM WITCH TRIALS WRITTEN BY BOSTON MINISTER COTTON MATHER, PUBLISHED IN 1692.)

ward her. That duty to provide both practical and spiritual care would now take on a new and extreme form.

Watching over a servant as she endured these strange fits was, to be sure, not as heart-wrenching for the Wescots as it had been to tend their own daughter when she went through similar torments. Yet it did distress them to see Kate—or indeed anyone—in such agony. They could hardly send the young woman away, as they had Joanna, to escape the evil eye of whoever was bewitching her: Kate was their servant and they could not spare her labor. Nor could they simply turn her out. Abigail Wescot trusted Kate a good deal less than did her husband, but the couple did agree that as master and mistress it was their duty to see her through this ordeal.

That duty involved protecting Kate from the physical torments and insidious overtures of the creatures afflicting her. Sometimes those who fell victim to supernatural assaults harmed themselves or others during their fits. Clearly she could not be left alone. Abigail would have to keep an eye on her as Kate dressed and made ready for breakfast. Watching her during meals was easy enough. But she would also have to be supervised closely while doing her household chores. Whenever Kate went outside to work in the yard, someone must accompany her. And night would bring no reprieve, for during the hours of darkness she was constantly afflicted by strange visions and torments. One night she had near forty such episodes.

The Wescots followed their pastor's instructions, but their close observation of Kate disrupted completely their routine duties, while their constant dread of her next fit played havoc with their nerves. Husband and wife were soon exhausted. After consulting with his wife, Daniel decided to ask their neighbors for help in keeping watch over Kate so that he and Abigail could get some rest. Neighbors could also help his wife to cope while he was away from home. Though the timing was unfortunate,

Daniel had to leave on a trip to Hartford, over sixty-five miles away.

The Wescots' neighbors responded readily. To request assistance in time of need was customary and expected in a place like Stamford. At harvest the men would help each other gather their crops; women would often meet in each other's households to give help and companionship as they spun and wove, prepared to give birth, and struggled through illness. These were, in a very practical sense, communities of households, sharing labor, exchanging goods, and providing Christian fellowship.

But Daniel Wescot had other reasons for calling in his neighbors. They could confirm that something supernatural was indeed plaguing his home. Daniel knew that some neighbors suspected Kate of feigning her fits and he did not want it put about that he was being duped by his own maid. Besides, if neighbors shared in watching over Kate, they could help identify the witches afflicting her. Kate's descriptions of the women who came to her during the fits were so far very hazy, but Daniel was determined to ferret them out. He thought he knew who might have tormented his daughter several years ago. Might not the same person be involved in his servant's bewitchment? If Daniel had witnesses to confirm Kate's reports or, better still, if the watchers themselves saw women entering the house as afflicting specters, that would strengthen his hand, should he seek to prosecute the malefactors.

Daniel Wescot had no intention of letting Kate's tormentors get away with their attacks. Left unchecked, the afflictions might spread to other members of his household. It would break his heart if Joanna's fits returned; and there were the other children to consider. Whoever was bewitching Kate might well be doing it to spite him and his wife rather than Kate herself. If so, the witches had to be stopped before they tired of tormenting the servant and went after his own kin.

It was over twenty years since anyone had been tried for witchcraft in Connecticut, but Daniel remembered hearing that an Irish woman had been hanged for witchcraft in Boston just a few years ago. He wanted the witches responsible for his household's afflictions punished and he wanted to be rid of them. "Thou shalt not suffer a witch to live." That was, after all, God's Word.

David Selleck was feeling extremely anxious by the time he and Abraham Finch arrived at the Wescots' house to watch over Katherine Branch through the night. Mister Wescot and his wife looked worn and tense, which did nothing to calm David's nerves as he and Abraham sat with the Wescots and drank a cup of cider. The rituals of hospitality over and done with, the master of the house led them up to the room where Kate was sleeping.

Mister Wescot told his neighbors they would need to take turns keeping watch over Kate as she slept. Someone had to be within easy reach to restrain her once the fits began and David agreed to go first, if only to get it over with. He settled on the narrow bed, just a few inches away from the young woman. He could hear her breathing, but she gave no other sign of life. Abraham sat nearby, gazing apprehensively at nothing in particular. It had been an arduous day and David felt tired, but there was no danger of him falling asleep—he felt far too tense.

Suddenly the Wescots' youngest daughter cried out in another room. David sat up in alarm and glanced down at Kate; thankfully, she was still asleep. Abraham crept out to investigate and returned a few minutes later. Nothing more than a bad dream, he reported, and her parents were calming her down.

When the time came for David to be relieved, he carried a light into the adjoining room, where he paced to and fro, unable to relax. All of a sudden he heard Kate scream and rushed back into her room. There he found Abraham sitting up on the bed, deathly pale, with Kate lying across his feet in what seemed to be a dead faint.

"She cried out," Abraham said, "and when I looked up I saw a ball of fire as big as my two hands pass across the room to the hearth, and then it disappeared."

Minutes later Kate came to her senses and they asked her why she had screamed. A woman had come into the room, she said, a woman with fiery eyes.

Once Kate settled down again, David took another turn lying beside her. Abraham, still shaken, lay on a chest nearby. Not long afterward David felt a pricking in his side that caused him to start. Abraham asked what had happened and he answered, "she pricked me."

"No, I didn't," Kate retorted, "it was Goody Crump."

Before either man could ask who that was, Kate held her hand over the side of the bed, palm open, and said, "Give me that thing that you pricked Mr. Selleck with!"

She then closed her hand. Abraham took hold of it, opened it up, and found a pin, which he removed. Kate's hand had been empty when she stretched it over the side of the bed, he would swear it. Both men were now completely unnerved.

A few nights later, Ebenezer Bishop, another of the Wescots' neighbors, was sitting beside Kate's bed when she suddenly called out: "Goody Clawson! Goody Clawson!"

Staring intently at what seemed to be an empty corner of the room, Kate declared, "Goody Clawson, turn head over heels!"

After this she had a violent fit and cried out at the top of her voice, "Now they're going to kill me! They're pinching me on the neck!"

Ebenezer took the light, leaned over from where he was sitting, and examined the young woman's neck. He could see a red mark about the same size as a large coin. Shortly afterward Kate cried out that they were pinching her again and pointed to her shoulder, where he could now see another red patch.

A few hours later both marks turned black and blue as though she had been bruised. But who or what had done this to Kate? Ebenezer had been sitting right beside her. He knew that no visible force had caused those marks. Any doubts he may have had that Kate was under an evil hand faded as he observed the marks on her neck and shoulder darken to a stark, menacing color while she slept fitfully.

Joseph Garnsey offered to spend time at the Wescots' house while Mister Wescot was away in Hartford, partly as a gesture of neighborly support but also because he was curious to see the maidservant's fits for himself. How could he not, after hearing the descriptions of Kate's torments that were circulating through the neighborhood? Abraham Finch had told him of the fireball. And the stories of her physical contortions were equally amazing. Samuel Holly, another neighbor who had watched over Kate, told Joseph that the young woman's breasts inflated like bladders and then suddenly collapsed into her body, soon afterward filling out again. "And there was a great rattling in her throat as if she was choking," Samuel added. "Believe me, all that I saw was beyond nature."

Mister Wescot himself claimed that during one of her fits Kate stuck out her tongue to a great length. "I put it back into her mouth again," he said, "and then looked in her mouth, and could see no tongue but what looked like a lump of flesh down her throat."

Kate's master also described how on one occasion she had been lying on the bed and was suddenly flung up against the headboard. He had not been paying attention at that instant and so did not see her rise up, but, hearing a noise, he turned toward the bed and saw her coming down. Minutes later it happened again. This time he saw her go up and down, with no apparent means of propulsion. Another time Kate was lying on the bed and then suddenly sprang up without the help of her hands or feet, landing on the floor six feet from the bed. Joseph had heard many stories of bewitchment, but none to equal this. Surely such occurrences were "beyond nature."

Yet Joseph had also heard talk about Kate's fits being counterfeit. Sarah Kecham told him about an experiment that she and several others had witnessed. After watching Kate lie in a stupor and then suddenly scream out in terror, Thomas Asten had declared that he was sure she was bewitched. Sarah disagreed, saying she did not believe there to be any witch in the town. Goodman Asten replied, "I've heard it said that if a person is bewitched, you can take a sword and hold it over them and they will laugh themselves to death."

He took a sword and held it over Kate, whereupon she burst into laughter. Sarah whispered that Kate might have laughed simply because she knew that the sword was being held over her and Mister Wescot, who was present, signaled Goodman Asten to repeat the experiment in such a way that the servant would not know the sword was there. This time she neither laughed nor changed her expression in any way.

Joseph also wondered about Daniel Wescot's role in his servant's supposed affliction. Rumor had it that Nathaniel and Abigail Cross had confronted Mister Wescot with the charge that Kate was counterfeiting her torments, to which he replied, "I'll venture both my cows against a calf that she'll do a trick tomorrow morning that nobody else can." Goody Cross had wanted to know what Daniel Wescot meant by that remark. "Can you make her do it when you want?" she asked. "Yes," he declared, "when I want I can make her do it." Did Mister Wescot have some kind of control over his servant's fits? Or was he trying to make people believe that? And if so, why?

Joseph decided to see the afflictions for himself and so volunteered to watch over Kate in company with Nathaniel Wyatt. At first the young woman went about her chores as if nothing was wrong. Joseph was unsure whether to feel relieved or disappointed. Then she went into the yard to fetch some clothes that were drying and the two men followed. All of a sudden Kate collapsed. Joseph carried her hastily into the house and laid her on a bed. She lay there motionless as if in a trance. Joseph prepared to sit with her in case she began to have fits and needed to be restrained, but Nathaniel had other plans. "There are some who think she dissembles," he reminded Joseph. "Now's our chance to make trial of that." True enough, especially since Mister Wescot was away and could not meddle.

The two men got permission from Mistress Wescot to carry out an experiment. Nathaniel, standing next to the bed, asked Joseph for a sharp knife. No sooner had Joseph reached for one than Kate came to her senses, jumped up, and ran outside to the henhouse. The two men smiled at each other: if Kate was truly senseless, how could she know that they were about to cut her and so run away to prevent them from hurting her? But their smiles vanished as they heard Kate's piercing scream. Joseph ran out to her and demanded to know what had happened.

"I'm in such pain that I cannot live," she declared and then fell into a paralyzed stupor. They carried her back into the house, stiff as a board, and again laid her on the bed. Joseph took up the knife a second time, determined not to be fooled by the young woman. As he brandished it, Kate again sprang to life, crying out, "You're going to cut me!" She then lay down again and said, "I'll tell you how it is with me. I'm possessed by the Devil and he appeared to me in the henhouse in the shape of a black calf. He wants me to be a witch and if I will not he'll tear me in pieces." The two men glanced at each other. Did she really expect them to believe this? But then Kate screamed again, pointing toward the window. "I see him! There he is!" As Joseph looked in that direction, he was startled to see a light dart into the house and across the room. Nathaniel had clearly also seen it and was equally astonished.

"Kate," asked Joseph, "what else have you seen?"

"The Devil's appeared to me in the shape of a white dog," she replied, "and in the shape of three women."

"Are the three women witches?"

"I cannot tell. They might be honest women for all I know, or they might be witches."

Joseph stared at Kate, uncertain what to think. If she was truly bewitched, were these women the witches who were afflicting her? And if so, what could be done to stop them?

· Two ·

WHO IS IT THAT
TORMENTS HER?

DANIEL AND ABIGAIL WESCOT'S HOME HAD BECOME THE STAGE
for a grim and perplexing drama. At its center was the luridly
physical and yet mystifying spectacle of Katherine Branch's fits.
Around the young woman there crowded a growing cast of characters, all determined to figure out who or what was causing her
fits. The residents of Stamford were anything but hasty in concluding that witchcraft must be responsible for Kate's torments:
differing points of view jostled and competed for ascendancy. At
first, not even the Wescots assumed that their servant was bewitched. Their first step was to call in the local medical expert,
not the town minister: they began by seeking a natural cause for
Kate's afflictions. Even once the Wescots became convinced that
witches were in fact causing the young woman's torments, not
all of their neighbors followed suit: some suspected that Kate was
faking her symptoms. Those who believed that she was under an
evil hand, and those who did not, were equally determined to
justify their points of view. Their approach was experimental:

they converged upon the Wescots' home and turned it into a laboratory of the occult with Kate as the specimen under investigation. They watched her; they tested her; and they reached conclusions based on what they observed.

Daniel and Abigail Wescot knew that they could not take effective action against the witches afflicting Kate without the help of their neighbors. If the malign intruders were to be identified and tried for their crimes, the Wescots would need supportive testimony. Mister and Mistress Wescot encouraged their neighbors to visit them, partly because they needed help looking after Kate but also to let other folks see for themselves the maidservant's ghastly symptoms and hear her accusations. Any visitor to their home was now a potential witness in court.

Katherine Branch's torments were impressive and a growing number of townsfolk had become convinced that she was indeed bewitched. Yet even those who agreed that Kate's afflictions were the result of witchcraft reacted in different ways. Stamford's pastor, John Bishop, saw the situation largely in terms of a spiritual struggle: he warned the young woman that Satan wanted to lure her into his service; the Devil's minions might promise to end her agonies if she succumbed, but she must resist or else face the greater torments of hell. He and neighboring ministers promised to pray that God would give Kate the strength to withstand the Devil's advances. The Wescots appreciated Mister Bishop's support, but focused their own energies on the practical challenge of removing the human witches who were apparently causing Kate's affliction. Their next task was to discover who was tormenting their servant and making her unfit to carry out her duties. They wanted to end Kate's ordeal as quickly as possible, for their sake as much as for hers, and they wanted those responsible to be made incapable of ever again afflicting a member of their household.

At first Kate was extremely vague in describing those who tormented her, but about three weeks after the fits began, she became much more informative. Kate told the Wescots that she had seen the specter of a woman in the house wearing a silk hood and a blue apron. That evening, she went out of doors, apparently calm in spirits, but a few moments later ran back inside, clearly terrified, and grabbed Daniel Wescot around his waist. When he asked her what had happened, Kate told him that she had seen an old woman at the door with two firebrands in her forehead. Her master asked what kind of clothes the woman wore. Kate said that the woman was wearing two homespun coats, one tucked up around her, the other hanging down.

It was on the following day that Kate first named one of the women afflicting her: Goody Clawson. This revelation came as no surprise to the Wescots. Elizabeth Clawson, a woman in her early sixties, had lived in Stamford with her husband Stephen ever since their marriage in 1655. Goody Clawson was suspected by many of having occult powers and of using them against her enemies. She was no friend of the Wescots. The Wescots had quarreled with Goody Clawson almost a decade before over the weight of some flax that she had supplied to them. Stamford's barter economy depended on the exchange of goods and labor. Flax, a fiber, was used to make cloth and also wicks for candles and lamps.

Since their disagreement over the flax, Goody Clawson had carried a grudge against the Wescots, especially Abigail, and leapt at any opportunity to insult her. On one occasion, as Kate's mistress passed by the Clawsons' house, Goody Clawson came outside and threw stones at her. Abigail Wescot had good reason to believe that Clawson resented the status that she enjoyed as the wife of a prominent householder. Mistress Wescot was one day visiting the home of Stephen Clawson, Jr., when Goody Clawson followed her into the house, demanded to know why she did not visit her, and then became verbally abusive. "Proud slut!" she declared. "You're fond of your fine clothes and you love to be mistress, but you never will be mine!"

It was soon after this altercation that the Wescots' eldest daughter Joanna began to suffer from strange pains and nightmarish visions. At the time, the Wescots had suspected that their vicious and vindictive neighbor was somehow responsible for Joanna's afflictions. It now appeared that she was turning her bile against their servant.

"There she is," Kate cried, "sitting on the spinning wheel!" Later she saw Clawson perched on the back of a chair. "I'm sure you are a witch," she declared, "else you could not sit so."

During the days that followed, the woman whom Kate named as Goodwife Clawson appeared to her over and over again. On one such occasion the afflicted servant declared, "Goody Clawson, let's have a turn, heels over head. Shall you go first, or shall I?"

A brief silence followed. "Well, if I go first, you shall do it after." And having said that, Kate turned heels over head two or three times and lay down on the floor, saying, "Come, if you won't do it, I'll beat your head against the wall!" Having spoken these words, Kate got up and looked around. "She's gone," she declared, and then fell into convulsions.

On another occasion Kate described the woman's attire in detail. Mister Wescot went outside immediately after Kate had spoken and saw Goodwife Clawson in the street, dressed exactly as Kate had described.

Soon after, Kate cried out during one of her fits that she could see a second specter in the form of a short and lame old woman. She called her "hook backed" and "crump backed." This woman wore a homespun coat with a waistcoat underneath and a black cap. Kate confirmed the description on returning to her senses and the Wescots soon decided that the lame woman must be Goody Miller: she was, after all, the only person in Stamford who fit Kate's description. Why Goody Miller wanted to bewitch their servant was a mystery since they had never quarreled with her and nor to their knowledge had Kate.

During the weeks that followed, several neighbors watching over Kate reported that they also heard her name Goody Miller, sometimes calling her "Goody Crump" or "Goody Hipshod." David Selleck and Abraham Finch watched in horror as Kate cried out during one of her fits, "Goody Miller, hold up your arm higher that the black dog may suck you better. Now I'm sure you are a witch for you've got a long teat under your arm." Both David and Abraham had heard that witches fed demonic spirits in the form of animals—just as mothers fed their infant children, except that witches used a third nipple hidden somewhere on their bodies and nourished the familiars with blood, not milk. Once Kate came to her senses, the two men asked her what she had seen during her fit. She answered that she saw Goody Miller give suck to a black dog and that the witch had a long teat under her arm.

Soon after Kate first named Goody Clawson and Goody Crump, Daniel Wescot had to leave for Hartford to attend a meeting of the colony's representative assembly. During his absence, Kate was disturbed again by cats, one of which turned into a third woman.

"Are you sure they were cats?" Abigail Wescot asked. "Couldn't it have been your fancy?"

"They were cats," Kate answered firmly.

"Well," declared Mistress Wescot, "if they be cats they are no ordinary cats for ordinary cats can't turn themselves into a woman and then into a cat again. What sort of a woman was it that you saw?"

"She was a pretty tall woman."

"What was she wearing?"

"Woolen cloth, the best quality homespun."

"Was there anything unusual about her face?"

"Not really."

"What about her mouth?"

"I think she had pretty thick lips."

Abigail Wescot saw that Kate's eyes were once again glazing over: she was clearly no longer in her right senses. Mistress Wescot turned to Joseph Bishop, a neighbor who was also present in the room. She presumed that she could speak to him freely without Kate hearing.

"I know a woman at Fairfield who was suspected formerly; she has thick lips. I suppose you know who I mean: Mercy Holbridge."

Kate started and gasped, "There she is again."

Mistress Wescot and her neighbor watched as Kate proceeded to ask the specter who she was. There followed a short silence, after which Kate announced that the woman's name was Mercy Woodbridge, but then she paused. After a moment Kate said that she had misheard the name and that it was really Mercy Holbridge. She went on to ask where the woman lived. The specter replied that she lived at Compo. When Kate came out of her fit, she asked her mistress where Compo was. Abigail Wescot replied grimly that it was a village just outside Fairfield.

Mistress Wescot knew Mercy Holbridge's history. Originally from New Haven, she was now a resident of Compo and in her early fifties. The family was trouble. Mercy's father, Arthur Holbridge, had been charged with theft and shady business dealings. Mercy had also been presented in court for various misdemeanors; Abigail recalled that Daniel had at one time given testimony against her. When Arthur Holbridge died, he left his family poverty-stricken and they became a charge upon the community. Mercy's life had changed for the better when she married Thomas Disborough of Compo, but she was known to be a difficult and vindictive neighbor. This was not the first time that Mercy had been suspected of witchcraft.

Several days later when Daniel Wescot returned home from Hartford, he made Kate repeat her description of this third woman.

"What does she look like?"

"She's of middle stature with thick lips." Mistress Wescot may well have noted the discrepancy between this answer and Kate's earlier description of the witch as a tall woman, though the thick lips did conform with what she had said before—and also with Abigail's own suspicions. Mister Wescot meanwhile continued his interrogation.

"How old is she?"

"Neither old nor young. She has on a dirty shift and a dirty cap."

"And where does she live?"

"Compo. I've been to Compo." This last remark doubtless perplexed Mistress Wescot. When Kate first spoke to the specter, she had not known where Compo was. Yet now she claimed to have been there.

Kate seemed to know that this third woman was no stranger to the Wescot household. "Mercy," she cried out during one of her fits, "why do you meddle with me? I never did you any wrong. What's it to me if my master did?" Once Kate emerged from the fit, Daniel Wescot asked her why she had spoken in that way.

"The woman told me that you wronged her in giving evidence against her." When she next went into a fit, Kate conversed again with the woman. "Why do you meddle with me? What's it to me if my master did that? But I've told him of it and he said nothing. I believe you lie."

Kate had now named three women. It was almost five weeks since the onset of her fits and her master decided that the time had come to act. Daniel Wescot lodged a formal complaint on behalf of his servant and appeared with her before a preliminary court of inquiry on the twenty-seventh of May 1692. The court consisted of four local magistrates: Jonathan Bell and Jonathan Selleck, both of whom lived in Stamford, along with two men from nearby Fairfield, John Burr and Nathan Gold. Their task was to determine whether the evidence that Mister Wescot presented justified a formal prosecution. Trials were time consuming, costly, and not to be undertaken lightly. Preliminary courts of inquiry could identify accusations that were frivolous or for which there was little supporting evidence; they could dismiss cases there and then, or they could determine that a full-scale trial should go ahead.

The magistrates met with Mister Wescot and his maidservant at the Stamford meetinghouse, the same building in which religious services and town meetings took place. The meetinghouse was a simple thirty-eight-foot-square timber building with a steep roof, built two decades ago to replace a smaller structure that the town had outgrown. Since then the population had continued to expand and the town had recently installed additional seating. The wooden benches were austerely functional and there was little decoration such as one would see in an English parish church or a Catholic chapel. The meetinghouse was a straightforward, multipurpose structure. Daniel Wescot would have been used to spending time in the building for town meetings as well as for church services, though never before had he come there for a purpose such as this.

Mister Selleck and his fellow magistrates asked Kate if she knew who it was that afflicted her. She replied without hesitation that she did.

"I've seen Goody Clawson sitting on a spinning wheel and on the back of a chair. This very day I've also seen Goody Hipshod."

"Who?"

"That's what I call her. I saw her sitting on the bedhead."

"Have you seen any other?"

"Yes, a woman who used to be called Mercy Holbridge but is now Mercy Disborough."

"How do you know her name?"

"She told me. She lives at Compo."

"How do you know that?"

"I've been there."

One of the magistrates asked her how she got there.

"I went on foot," Katherine explained, "and Mercy was my guide, there and back again."

Mister Wescot doubtless listened intently to this explanation. He had probably heard from his wife about the inconsistency in Kate's remarks about Compo: at first, in conversation with Mistress Wescot, she had said that she did not know where Compo was; later, when questioned by Mister Wescot, she claimed to have been there. It now transpired that their servant had recently visited Compo in secret with Mercy Disborough, which would explain the apparent discrepancy. It was hardly reassuring, though, to learn that their servant was being led hither and thither by witches. Kate had been in her right mind since she entered the meeting house and gave calm, confident answers to the magistrates' questions. But she now fell into another fit and the magistrates decided to end their interrogation, at least for the time being.

The very next day, Elizabeth Clawson and Mercy Disborough were brought before the court for questioning. Clawson's home was within walking distance of the meetinghouse, but Disborough had to be fetched from Compo. Both women insisted that they were innocent.

"You have been named by a servant maid of Mister Wescot's as having a hand in afflicting her by witchcraft," declared Jonathan Selleck. "Are you one of those who afflict her?"

"I absolutely deny that I am any such person," replied Clawson. Her tone, the magistrates would have noted disapprovingly, was abrupt and far from respectful. She acknowledged that there had been "a dissension" between her and the Wescots some eight or nine years since, but denied that she was now taking revenge for that quarrel.

"I know of no means whereby the maid is afflicted," she declared.

Mercy Disborough also spoke confidently and without hesitation.

"I never saw or knew of the girl before," she declared, "and never heard there was such a person in the world till now."

During Goody Disborough's examination, Kate was carried into the meeting house in a stupor. She came to her senses while Disborough was speaking and, endeavoring to raise herself up, asked, "Where is she?"

Mister Wescot helped Kate up and at that point Goody Disborough turned to face her. Kate immediately fell down into another fit. A few minutes later, she came to herself again and asked, "Where is Mercy? I hear her voice."

She had been lying with her face away from Goody Disborough, but now turned and saw her.

"It's her! I'm sure it's her!"

Kate straight away fell into another bout of convulsive fits.

The magistrates gave orders for both women to be placed "under restraint of authority." Mercy Disborough was sent to the county jail in Fairfield; Elizabeth Clawson remained in Stamford under house arrest for several weeks until she too was removed to Fairfield. Once they were "under restraint," Kate said that she could no longer see their specters. When the apparition of the woman whom she called Goody Hipshod next appeared to her, Kate asked mockingly where the other two witches were and then informed the specter that they had been apprehended. Goody Hipshod, she declared, would soon be joining them.

Just over a fortnight later, on 13 June, Daniel Wescot arrived with Katherine Branch at the house of Jonathan Selleck, one of the magistrates who had questioned her at the meetinghouse and who wished to examine Kate further. Mister Selleck was the wealthiest man in Stamford and his house doubtless reflected that. It was probably bigger than the Wescots' home and more expensively decorated. Some of the furniture may have been imported from England instead of being made locally and the woodwork would have been more elaborately carved than in most homes. The cut of Mister Selleck's clothes and the quality of fabric from which they were made would also have exhibited his social status. Kate may not have been inside the house previously: perhaps she was awed by the magistrate and his evident wealth; or perhaps she was too preoccupied with the task in hand

THE HOYT-BARNUM HOUSE IN STAMFORD, BUILT IN THE LATE SEVENTEENTH CENTURY AND NOW RESTORED TO ITS ORIGINAL CONDITION *Like most houses in New England, this one was built of wood; the framework consisted of posts and beams held together by wooden pins. The house had a stone foundation, and the chimney was also made from stones bonded by a mortar consisting of clay, animal hair, and straw.* (SOURCE: THIS PHOTOGRAPH IS REPRODUCED BY KIND PERMISSION OF THE STAMFORD HISTORICAL SOCIETY.)

to take much notice of her surroundings. After all, she had a story to tell.

Kate told Mister Selleck that since her first examination four more women had appeared to her: a girl and her mother who both lived in Fairfield but whose names she did not know; a woman from New York who called herself Mary Glover; and another woman from Boston, whom the girl from Fairfield named as Goody Abison. Since Elizabeth Clawson and Mercy Disborough had been arrested, Kate added, they had come only once in the night to afflict her. But Goody Miller had tormented her repeatedly, along with these other women. Kate claimed that she was not their only victim: last night, she declared, Goody Miller and Goody Abison had dragged one of Mister Wescot's children out of bed and along the floor.

A woman named Mary Glover had indeed been accused of witchcraft in 1688, but she had lived in Boston, not New York, and was hanged that same year. Where was Kate getting her information? Mister Selleck asked Kate if her master or mistress or any other person had mentioned in her hearing any of the persons whom she now accused of tormenting her. Kate answered that she had never heard their names until the apparitions themselves told her who they were. Mister Selleck then asked Kate if she would take an oath as to the truth of what she said, especially her claim that nobody had mentioned the persons she accused before the specters themselves gave her the names. Kate answered that she would do so willingly.

At the end of June, Daniel Wescot brought Kate back to tell Jonathan Selleck about her most recent afflictions. Neighbors crowded into the house, some doubtless drawn by sympathy for Kate's plight, others by the thrilling prospect of witnessing one of her attacks. The room was thick with anticipation.

Kate told Mister Selleck that Goody Clawson had reappeared last Saturday night and tormented her more grievously than ever. "She held my head back, pulling my arms, and pressed upon me, causing me much pain." Daniel Wescot now stepped in to confirm and elaborate on his servant's account. "She made a terrible screeching noise," he declared. "She cried out, 'Goody Clawson, Goody Clawson, why will you kill me? Why will you torment me?' Her head was bent backward and when I went to lift her up she seemed three times heavier than her normal weight. The maid cried out, 'Get off me!' several times. When she came to her senses, I asked her who was tormenting her and she answered, 'Goody Clawson, Goody Clawson, Goody Clawson.' During her fit, she and the bedstead shook so hard that we were all much affrighted."

The torments had been repeated the following night, though not to such extremes. Then Elizabeth Clawson was finally removed from Stamford and sent away to be kept with Mercy Disborough at the jail in Fairfield, since when, Kate declared, she had been afflicted only by Goody Miller.

Once Mister Selleck finished questioning Kate, she left the house, accompanied by his Indian servant. But a few minutes later the Indian reappeared: Kate had got some three hundred yards from the house when she suddenly fell down in a fit. Mister Selleck's son John and David Selleck, a cousin, went outside and carried Kate back to the house, stiff as a board. Coming out of her stupor, she screamed and cried out, "Goody Clawson, you kill me! Goody Clawson, you kill me!" Kate's head was bent backward, her arm twisted around to her back.

"You're breaking my arm," she cried and fell into such violent fits that two men could scarcely restrain her, to the amazement of those still gathered in the house.

Daniel Wescot and Jonathan Selleck decided not to move Kate until the following morning. All night long her torments continued. During brief gaps between spasms of agony she conversed with the apparitions. "Goody Clawson," she asked in a woebegone tone, "why do you torment me so? I never did you any harm in word or deed. Why are you all come now to afflict me?"

A little later she declared, "I will not yield, for you are witches and your portion is hellfire to all eternity. Mister Bishop has often told me I must not yield and the minister from Norwalk has said the same, so I hope God will keep me from yielding to you."

Kate named five women whose specters she conversed with that night: Elizabeth Clawson, Mercy Disborough, Goody Miller, the little girl, and her mother. The girl she now addressed as Sarah.

"Is Sarah Staples your right name? I'm afraid you tell me a lie. Tell me your right name!"

This she repeated several times before declaring, "Yes, I must tell my master and Mister Selleck if they ask me, but I'll tell no one else."

A short silence.

"Hannah Harvey? Is that your name? Then why did you tell me a lie before? Well then, what is the name of the woman who comes with you?"

Another silence.

"Yes, I must tell my master and Mister Selleck if he asks me, but I'll tell no one else. You will not tell me? Then I will ask Goody Crump."

"Goody Crump," she said, turning in another direction, "what is the name of the woman who comes with Hannah Harvey?" She asked this several times and then declared, "Mary! Mary what? Mary Harvey? Well then, is Mary Harvey the mother of Hannah Harvey? Now I know it! Why did you not tell me before? There were more cats came at first, and I shall know all your names. What creature is that with a great head and wings and no body and all black? Hannah, is that your father? I believe it is, for you are a witch. Hannah, what is your father's name? And have you no grandfather and grandmother? How came you to be a witch?"

She stopped again and then resumed after listening carefully.

"A grandmother? What is her name?" Another pause.

"Goody Staples? What was her maiden name?"

Mister Selleck most likely knew that the husband of a New Haven woman named Mary Staples had won a slander suit many years before against a neighbor who accused her of being a witch and a liar. It had been an ugly business. Goodwife Staples had angrily confronted the neighbor in church. Many witnesses, including the local minister, later testified in court for one side or the other. Staples had a daughter Mary whose married name was Harvey; Mary had a daughter named Hannah.

Mister Selleck's attention was drawn back to Kate's fits. She began to sing songs and hum tunes, "gigs for them to dance by," as she said. She then recited a great many religious verses and also the dialogue between Christ and the Devil as well as the Lord's Prayer, the Commandments, and the Catechism (an outline of Puritan faith in the form of questions and answers that children in godly households learned by heart).

Early the following morning Jonathan Selleck wrote to Nathan Gold, who had presided with him over the initial inquiry. "Yesterday," he reported, "Mister Wescot brought his maid Kate down to my house to be examined, and I took her relation concerning how she had been afflicted of late, which is too long to relate, but I refer you to the bearer of this letter, my son John Selleck, who was a spectator with several others at the time. The poor girl was forced to stay all night and as yet has not come to her senses. But when she does I shall examine her about what she discoursed in her fits. She said in her fits last night that there was a creature she saw among them with a great head and wings, all black, and Kate asked the girl she called Hannah if it was her father. I believe it is. What this may mean the Lord knows. I fear that all the persons she has named are wicked and I desire the Lord to make discovery of them."

When Kate came to her senses that morning, Jonathan Selleck questioned her about the previous evening's ordeal. She described again the torments inflicted by Elizabeth Clawson, Mercy Disborough, Goody Miller, and Mary and Hannah Harvey. "They were terribly mad at me for telling things against them."

Kate began to weep quietly. No flailing and screaming, thought Mister Selleck, no drama and spectacle . . . just a frightened and exhausted young woman. Something truly horrifying must be causing such anguish. It was his responsibility to protect her and to punish those responsible. Such was his duty as a neighbor, as a fellow Christian, and as an officer of the law. Daniel Wescot had placed his trust in him by bringing the maid repeatedly to his house so that he could attest to her fits, question her, and act on her allegations. Mister Selleck did not intend to betray that trust.

Jonathan Selleck knew that other residents of Stamford also suspected Goody Clawson of witchcraft and he had heard of the suspicions surrounding Goody Disborough in Compo. But how exactly would the Lord "make discovery of them" in such a way that their crimes could be proven in a court of law? And what of those neighbors who refused to believe in Elizabeth Clawson's guilt and were already mobilizing on her behalf? Ahead lay legal and political thickets that he was glad not to be facing alone.

· *Three* ·

"By the Law of God and the Law of the Colony Thou Deservest to Die"

As magistrate Jonathan Selleck pondered the chilling scenes that he had witnessed over the past few weeks, he became increasingly worried about the dangers facing Stamford. Mister Selleck had spent his entire adult life in the town and was regarded as one of its foremost residents. Though born in Boston, he and his younger brother John had moved to Connecticut in 1660. Jonathan was twenty at the time, John seventeen. The two brothers became partners in trade, following in the footsteps of their father, a merchant who had traveled down to Barbados regularly until his death in 1654. Jonathan was the more sedentary of the two; it was John who ferried their cargo back and forth, spending weeks and sometimes months away at sea. The town, realizing that it stood to benefit from the Selleck brothers' commercial ventures, had granted them land for a warehouse.

Within a decade of their arrival the two brothers married two sisters, Abigail and Sarah Law, daughters of a wealthy townsman.

Each received a house as dowry. Jonathan soon became an officer in Stamford's militia and was given more land by the town as thanks for his leadership in the war against the Indians in 1676. He served regularly as an elected representative at the colonial assembly and for several years as a member of the governor's council. The brothers purchased real estate in the area and inherited yet more land on the death of their father-in-law in 1686, becoming major property owners in and around Stamford.

The brothers' mercantile business had prospered until 1689, when John and his ship were captured by the French, who had just declared war on England and its colonies—he was never heard from again. Jonathan was still reeling from this personal and financial blow, but he would not allow the family's maritime business, built up over many years, to be undermined by this French outrage and so he had recently joined with one of his sons and three other men to buy a replacement vessel.

Jonathan Selleck had become a key player in local affairs and had close ties to the countywide network of leading families. It was becoming increasingly clear, much to Jonathan's delight, that his two sons would marry the daughters of Nathan Gold, a good friend and prominent citizen in Fairfield. Nathan Gold had sat with Jonathan Selleck on the preliminary court of inquiry investigating Katherine Branch's accusations; both men felt a keen sense of responsibility to defend Stamford against the threat posed by witches.

Yet how best to protect the town? Mister Selleck was well aware that allegations of witchcraft could multiply rapidly and plunge entire communities into crisis. In the early 1660s, soon after he and his brother moved to Connecticut, a witch scare in

Hartford had resulted in formal indictments against eleven people. That investigation also began with mysterious fits that were blamed on local women. The Hartford witch hunt had become part of local lore. It now seemed darkly familiar in light of Kate's torments and recent reports from Massachusetts, where a wave of afflictions and accusations threatened to engulf an entire county. Those reports were not encouraging as Jonathan Selleck and his fellow magistrates launched their own investigation. Mister Selleck knew that long-festering suspicions could resurface on such occasions. Mary Staples was a case in point: many years had passed since she sought restitution for being slandered as a witch, yet now the rumors were back to haunt her in old age. Katherine Branch claimed that the specter of Hannah Harvey had named Hannah's grandmother, Mary Staples, as a witch.

Jonathan Selleck also knew that trying to prove an invisible crime in court was not easy and could lead to serious problems, both inside and outside the courtroom. Religious doctrine and the legal code invited accusations of witchcraft, yet court officials were often much less impressed by the evidence presented in such cases than were the accusers and their supporters. Ministers, magistrates, and ordinary townsfolk agreed that witches posed a real and serious threat, but agreeing on how to prove witchcraft in a court of law was quite another matter.

A number of controversial acquittals in Connecticut had caused friction between officials determined to uphold legal standards of proof and local residents convinced of a defendant's guilt. Of the eleven women and men indicted during the 1662–63 Hartford witch hunt, only four were convicted, to the dismay of those who believed them all to deserve death. A few years later, in 1665, another Hartford woman, Elizabeth Seager, was convicted of witchcraft by the jurymen charged with her case. But the governor refused to carry out the sentence, declaring the evidence inadequate. Goody Seager was subsequently freed on the grounds that the jury's decision to convict was legally indefensible. The jurymen were furious and those who believed that Elizabeth Seager was a witch, of whom there were many, made it clear that they felt betrayed. In 1668, Katherine Harrison of Wethersfield also escaped conviction after a prolonged and bitter trial. When the magistrates charged with that case overturned the jury's verdict and released the accused woman, they insisted that she leave Wethersfield permanently, both for her own safety and for her neighbors' peace of mind.

These acquittals doubtless pleased the accused and their supporters, but others were horrified. Elizabeth Seager's and Katherine Harrison's survival dealt a heavy blow to public trust in the legal system and its willingness to protect settlers from witches. Between 1669 and 1692, there had been no witch trials in Connecticut. Ordinary folk had by and large kept their suspicions of neighbors to themselves and magistrates had done nothing to discourage that. But now Daniel Wescot had unleashed a wave of public accusations as people came forward to testify against Elizabeth Clawson and Mercy Disborough—though not against the other women whom Kate had named. Mister Selleck may well have felt that he and his fellow magistrates were themselves on trial as local residents watched closely to see how they would handle the situation.

The magistrates' task was complicated by doubts and disagreement among residents of Stamford on the subject of Katherine

Branch. Jonathan Selleck knew that some locals suspected Kate of dissembling. As neighbors visited the Wescot home to observe Kate's torments, opinions as to her credibility became ever more divided. Joseph Garnsey and Nathaniel Wyatt both swore that Kate told them she was possessed by the Devil, yet Lydia Penoir told the magistrates that Kate later denied having said any such thing. Goody Penoir, who was Abigail Wescots' niece, heard her aunt declare that Kate was "such a lying girl that no one could believe a word she said." Mistress Wescot had also remarked— with an edge of bitterness in her voice, no doubt—that her husband would believe their maid over the pastor, or the town magistrates, or herself. "Neither Mercy, nor Goody Miller, nor Hannah, nor any of these women whom she impeaches, are any more witches than I am," proclaimed Mistress Wescot.

Daniel Wescot had apparently boasted that he could control Kate's convulsions. Some townsfolk wondered if he was also influencing whom she accused. Others suspected that Kate's naming of witches might have been influenced by her mistress. According to Joseph Bishop, Mistress Wescot told him in front of Kate that she thought Mercy Disborough was one of the women afflicting her. It was almost immediately after she made that remark that Kate named Goody Disborough. Mistress Wescot, confronted with the allegation that she was prompting her servant, replied that Kate was "in her fit" at the time and so could not hear her—she could tell from the way in which Kate's eyes glazed over. Not everyone found that explanation convincing.

Many townfolk were convinced that Kate was bewitched, but it did not necessarily follow that her allegations against specific women were reliable. Assuming that Kate was getting her infor-

DEPOSITION GIVEN BY LYDIA PENOIR AND DATED 24 AUGUST 1692, FROM THE SAMUEL WYLLYS PAPERS *The deposition reads as follows:*

"the testimony of Lidia penoir[:] shee saith that shee heard her a[u]nt abigail wescot say that her servant girl Catern branch was such a Lying gairl that not any boddy Could beleive one word what shee said and saith that shee heard her a[u]nt abigail wescot say that shee did not beleive that mearcy nor goody miller nor hannah nor any of these women whome shee had apeacht was any more witches then shee was and that her husband would beleive Catern before he would beleive mr bishop or Leiftenat bell or her self.

The test[at]or is Ready to give oath to s[ai]d testimony

Stanford
Aug[us]t 24[th] 1692"

mation from the specters afflicting her, could they be trusted? Ministers taught that specters were demons who assumed human form on instruction from Satan: when witches signed a covenant with him, the Devil agreed to send demons on request to torment their enemies. According to the clergy, witches had no occult power of their own; demons acted on their behalf, taking on the appearance of the witches for whom they acted. Most people assumed that a specter's appearance matched the identity of the witch who wanted to harm the victim. But might specters appear as innocent people so as to incriminate harmless and virtuous individuals? In Massachusetts, a growing number of ministers and magistrates—learned and great men—were casting doubt on whether information collected from demonic sources should be taken on faith. Was not Satan the father of lies? The court would need evidence that was untainted by the possibility of demonic fraud. Given that the crimes in question were occult in nature, such evidence might well prove hard to come by.

Jonathan Selleck and his fellow magistrates faced an additional problem. One of the accused, Goody Miller, heard that she had been named and promptly fled to Bedford, New York, where her two brothers lived. One was a magistrate, the other Bedford's chief military officer. This was a canny move on Goody Miller's part—and not just because her brothers were influential men who might be able to protect her. Several Stamford families had moved away to found Bedford in 1680. The distance between the two towns was only ten miles and Bedford, though close to the New York border, was at the time under Connecticut's jurisdiction. But in 1683 a revised boundary agreement shifted Bedford into New York. This meant that courts in Connecticut had no jurisdiction over Goody Miller, as long as she stayed with her brothers.

In June 1692 Daniel Wescot visited Bedford. He wanted the magistrates there to send Goody Miller back to Stamford for interrogation. But Goody Miller's brother refused even to question her, let alone order her removal. He told Daniel Wescot bluntly that he knew what would become of his sister if she returned to Connecticut. Another local magistrate agreed at first to arrange for Goody Miller's return, but changed his tune after consulting with her brothers. He did promise to discuss the matter with New York's attorney general, James Graham, but that gentleman also refused to cooperate (perhaps out of loyalty to Goody Miller's brothers or friends who had sided with them, perhaps because he was loathe to cooperate with Connecticut, or perhaps because he believed that Goody Miller was innocent).

Daniel Wescot was not alone in trying to influence officials across the border. Jonathan Selleck hoped to bring Goody Miller back through the personal intervention of Colonel Caleb Heathcott, an influential landowner in New York and a close friend of the governor. Jonathan Selleck and Caleb Heathcott had known each other since the early 1670s, but there were no guarantees that their acquaintance or Caleb Heathcott's friendship with the governor would ensure Goody Miller's extradition.

Meanwhile, preparations were underway to prosecute the five other women whom Kate had named: Elizabeth Clawson, Mercy Disborough, Mary Staples, Mary Harvey, and Hannah Harvey.

Capital offenses, including witchcraft, were tried by the Court of Assistants, a judicial body of twelve men elected each May by the colony's representative assembly. (Lesser crimes were tried in local county courts.) The Court of Assistants met in Hartford, Connecticut's center of government, some sixty-five miles away from Stamford. For people who lived in Stamford and Compo to make that journey in order to testify would mean an absence of several days from their farms and families, with all the inconvenience and expense that such a trip would involve. The logistics of transporting to Hartford all those who had volunteered information about the case would be daunting; the prospect of having to make that journey would most likely discourage other potential witnesses from coming forward.

There was an immediate precedent at hand for dealing with a situation like this. When the recent crisis in Salem had produced a deluge of accusations along with scores of witnesses, the Massachusetts governor appointed a special judicial commission to try the accused locally in Salem Town, even though Boston, the seat of government in Massachusetts, was much closer to Salem Village and the other affected communities than Hartford was to Stamford. Connecticut's representative assembly decided to follow the example set by its counterpart in Massachusetts and so on 22 June created a Court of Oyer and Terminer (meaning to "hear and determine"). The special court would meet in Fairfield to adjudicate the cases arising from Katherine Branch's accusations, "which are not so capable to be brought to a trial at the usual Court of Assistants by reason of the multiplicity of witnesses that may be concerned in the case." The court included Governor Robert Treat, Deputy Governor William Jones, and five of the Assistants, John Allyn, John Burr, Andrew Leete, Moses Mansfield, and William Pitkin—an impressive group that would surely inspire respect and confidence. Jonathan Selleck and the three other local magistrates who had presided over the initial court of inquiry may well have been relieved to hand over responsibility for these cases to the special court. In its hands now rested the fate of the accused women.

When the special court convened two and a half months later, in mid-September, the magistrates dealt swiftly with the allegations against Mary Staples, her daughter Mary Harvey, and her granddaughter Hannah Harvey. The depositions amassed throughout the summer included hardly any mention of these women, other than testimony from Katherine Branch and those who reported what she said. On Friday, 15 September, the Grand Jury presented Goody Staples, Goody Harvey, and little Hannah to the court on suspicion of witchcraft. The jurymen took the position that Kate's testimony was in and of itself sufficient to justify a trial, but the magistrates were reluctant to rely upon Kate's allegations: even if she herself was telling the truth about what the specters told her, they knew from the controversy brewing in Salem that this was a dangerous foundation on which to build a legal case.

The magistrates accordingly issued a formal proclamation that anyone with evidence against "the widow Mary Staples, Mary Harvey, the wife of Josiah Harvey, and Hannah Harvey" should come forward and would be heard. Only two witnesses appeared. Hester Grumman testified that during an illness that spring she had seen the specters of Mary Staples and Mercy Disborough in her room, dancing at the foot of her bed. John Tash told the court that some thirty years before he had taken Goody Staples on his horse from one town to another as a favor and that while they were crossing some swampy ground he became worried that she was no longer on the horse. Goody Staples was a light woman, to be sure, so he reached back and felt for her; there seemed to be no one there. Yet as soon as they were back on firm land he could feel her behind him again.

Goody Grumman and Goodman Tash clearly felt that their depositions should count as compelling evidence. Yet, as one of the magistrates put it, such anecdotes could carry "no great weight" in a court of law. The magistrates therefore decreed on Saturday, 16 September, that the three women should be set free. "The aforesaid persons," they declared, "are acquitted by proclamation, nothing of consequence appearing against them, and all persons are commanded to forebear speaking evil of the aforesaid persons for the future upon pain of displeasure."

The court could now focus its attention on Goody Clawson and Goody Disborough. The evidence relating to Elizabeth Clawson was by no means entirely one-sided. Many of Goody Clawson's neighbors refused to believe the allegations against her and had come forward to testify on her behalf. At the request of her husband, no fewer than seventy-six townsfolk (forty-eight men and twenty-eight women, including twenty-three couples) signed a petition of support. Among the women was Sarah Bates, the midwife who examined Kate soon after her fits began; Goody Bates now sided formally with those who rejected the servant's accusations against Goody Clawson. This was a sizeable group of Stamford residents, including many town leaders such as

Jonathan Bell, one of the magistrates who presided over the initial hearing in late May, and Abraham Ambler, who had over the years served as town selectman, town clerk, and representative to the colonial assembly. The petition, which was written in Abraham Ambler's hand and dated 4 June 1692, insisted that Goodwife Clawson did not have the temperament of a witch:

> Our neighbor Stephen Clawson having desired us whose names are under written, seeing there is such a report of his wife raised by some among us, that we would speak what we know concerning his said wife and her behavior among us for so many years. Now know all whom it may concern that we do declare that since we have known our said neighbor Goodwife Clawson we have not known her to be of a contentious frame nor given to use threatening words nor to act maliciously towards her neighbors, but hath been civil and orderly towards others and never a busybody in other men's concerns.

Eleazer Slawson and Clement Buxton also vouched for Goody Clawson in separate declarations. "I have always observed her," declared Goodman Slawson, "to be a person for peace and to counsel for peace and when she hath had provocations from her neighbors would answer and say, 'We must live in peace for we are neighbors,' and would never to my observation give threatening words, nor did I look at her as one given to malice."

Other neighbors, however, portrayed Elizabeth Clawson and Mercy Disborough as argumentative and vindictive. Following the arrest of the two women, a wave of Stamford and Compo residents came forward to relate quarrels with one or the other which had been followed by mysterious illness or misfortune. These witnesses were clearly convinced that Elizabeth Clawson and Mercy Disborough took revenge for disagreements or personal slights by bewitching the goods, cattle, or bodies of those who crossed them. The magistrates recognized that all of this testimony would have to be examined with great care. But at least they need not depend in these two cases on Katherine Branch's controversial testimony.

Both women reacted to the allegations against them in ways that seemed to incriminate them further. Just over a week after the initial court of inquiry first questioned Elizabeth Clawson, Daniel Wescot went to confront her about the bewitchment of his servant and her anger toward his family. "You told the magistrates that you never lay down to sleep in anger," he declared. " How can that be when you're still angry with me? Are you still angry with me?"

"What do you think?" Goody Clawson replied. That evening Kate's fits became more violent than they had been of late. Mistress Wescot, hearing her youngest daughter cry out, went into the room where she had been put to bed. The infant was lying on the floor near the hearth, at some distance from the bed. A large chair and chest placed beside the bed would have made it impossible for the infant girl to fall of her own accord. Daniel Wescot followed his wife into the room and found her sitting on the chair by the bed, her face contorted in anger and fear.

Having returned his daughter to her bed, Daniel Wescot went to lie with Kate to prevent her falling off the bed or being thrown to the floor. Kate took hold of his hair and pulled it hard. Daniel grabbed Kate's hands and held them firmly in his own. At that moment something whipped across his face like a cord; it smarted for some time after.

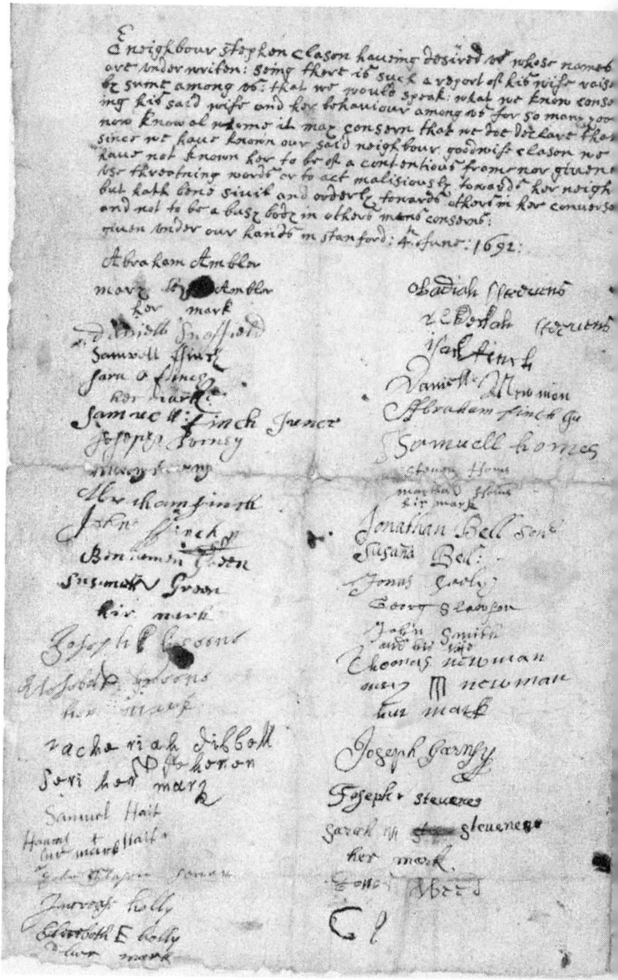

E neighbour Styphon Clason having desired us whose names are under writon: being that it is such a report of his wife raising his said wife and her behaviour among us for so many... [remainder of handwritten text illegible]

given under our hands in Stanford: 4 June: 1692:

Abraham Ambler
mary her mark Ambler
her mark
Samuell Finch
Sara ō Finch
her mark
Samuell Finch Juner
Joseph Finey
[illegible]
John Finch
Benjamin Goden
Susannah Green
her mark
Joseph Green
[illegible]
her mark
zachariah Dibboll
[illegible]
Seri her mark
Samuel Hait
Hannah her mark Hait
[illegible]
[illegible] Kelly
Elizabeth E Kelly
her mark

Obadiah [illegible]
[illegible]
Vast Finch
Daniell Newman
Abraham Finch Ju
Samuell homes
[illegible] Home
mary her mark Home
her mark
Jonathan Bell sen
Susana Bell
Jonas Cooly
Barty Clawson
Jogin Smith
and his wife
Thomas newman
mary M newman
her mark
Joseph Garnsy
Joseph + stevens
Sarah M stevens
her mark
[illegible] Mead

A PETITION ON BEHALF OF ELIZABETH CLAWSON, SIGNED BY SEVENTY-SIX STAMFORD RESIDENTS (FORTY-EIGHT MEN AND TWENTY-EIGHT WOMEN), DATED 4 JUNE 1692 *A majority of the women signed with a "mark" because they could not write their names;*

some of those who could not write may have been able to read, which
New Englanders saw as a higher priority because that enabled people to
read holy scripture. (SOURCE: REPRODUCED BY KIND PERMISSION OF THE
STAMFORD HISTORICAL SOCIETY.)

The Wescots did not believe it a coincidence that these new afflictions struck within a few hours of Daniel's conversation with Goody Clawson. The witches were evidently now coming after their own children. The next morning Daniel related this latest turn of events to Jonathan Selleck, so that it could be entered as evidence against Elizabeth Clawson once her trial began.

Mercy Disborough also made intemperate remarks following her arrest that deepened suspicions against her. Joseph Stirg and Benjamin Dunning visited Goody Disborough in the county jail. Benjamin asked if she was going to cooperate with the court and name the other witches working with her.

"Do you think," Mercy replied, laughing bitterly, "that I would be such a fool as to hang alone?"

Joseph declared that this amounted to an admission of guilt. Goody Disborough was, after all, suggesting that she knew other witches and could incriminate them, which meant that she herself was a witch. Mercy made no response. Perhaps she realized that she had made a tactical blunder and was now determined to keep quiet; perhaps she was too angry to say anything else. In any case, Joseph and Benjamin felt sure that the magistrates would be interested to hear about the accused woman's outburst and so they each submitted a deposition reporting the incident.

Thomas Halliberch, Mercy Disborough's jailkeeper, was completely baffled by some of her remarks. Mercy told him one morning that she had suffered terrible torments throughout the night. He replied that it must be the Devil, to which Mercy answered that she believed it was and that she had called on the Father, Son, and Holy Ghost for protection. The Devil told her that she had damned her soul and she feared as much, but hoped it was not so. "I put my trust in the Lord Jesus," Mercy declared. "If he has deceived me, I would not have others trust him. I believe that there's divination in all my troubles."

The jailkeeper wondered what his prisoner meant by this. Did she believe, or want him to believe, that she herself was bewitched? That she was trying to ward off evil forces? If she was not a witch, why was the Devil appearing to her? Did he want her to become a witch? Why was Mercy Disborough worried that she had damned herself? What did she mean by declaring that Christ might have deceived her? Was she trying to shift blame for giving way to the Devil's advances away from herself? Was she already a witch and trying to explain away a conversation with Satan that she feared others might have heard? Her words were highly suspicious, the jailor concluded, and so he relayed them to the court.

After reviewing the dozens of depositions against Elizabeth Clawson and Mercy Disborough, the magistrates decided to accept the Grand Jury's recommendation that they both be tried for witchcraft. Indictments were accordingly drawn up and issued:

Elizabeth Clawson, wife of Stephen Clawson of Stamford in the county of Fairfield in the colony of Connecticut, thou art here indicted by the name of Elizabeth Clawson that, not having the fear of God before thine eyes, thou hast had familiarity with Satan, the grand enemy of God and man, and that by his instigation and help thou hast in a preternatural way afflicted and done harm to the bodies and estates of sundry of their Majesties' subjects or to some of them contrary to the peace of our sovereign Lord the King and Queen, their crown and dignity, and that on the 25th April in the

4th year of their Majesties' reign and at sundry other times, for which by the law of God and the law of the colony thou deservest to die.

Mercy Disborough, wife of Thomas Disborough of Compo in Fairfield, thou art here indicted by the name of Mercy Disborough that, not having the fear of God before thine eyes, thou hast had familiarity with Satan, the grand enemy of God and man, and that by his instigation and help thou hast in a preternatural way afflicted and done harm to the bodies and estates of sundry of their Majesties' subjects or to some of them contrary to the peace of ye sovereign Lord the King and Queen, their crown and dignity, and that on the 25th April in the 4th year of their Majesties' reign and at sundry other times, for which by the law of God and the laws of this colony thou deservest to die.

Both defendants again declared themselves innocent. Both were committed to trial. If found guilty, both would be hanged. Whether or not that happened would depend in large part on the depositions given by neighbors in Stamford and Compo. Impressive though these depositions were in their sheer quantity, the magistrates and jurymen would need to pay close attention to the actual content. It was not enough to establish that people in Stamford and Compo believed the two women to be guilty. The evidence must satisfy specific criteria established by legal experts on both sides of the Atlantic. These criteria were far from straightforward and the magistrates responsible for overseeing the trials now faced three considerable challenges: first, to make sure that they themselves understood the established grounds for conviction in witchcraft cases and avoided the kinds of confusion that had plagued some trials in the past;

second, to ensure that the jurymen not only understood but also abided by those guidelines; and third, perhaps most daunting of all, to handle as diplomatically as possible the mounting public pressure for conviction. Many residents of Stamford and Compo were convinced of Elizabeth Clawson's and Goody Disborough's guilt; they had their own ideas as to what constituted proof; and they were not going to be pleased if the court viewed the situation differently.

· *Four* ·

ANGRY SPEECHES AND
STRANGE AFFLICTIONS

JOHN FINCH WORE A GRIM, IMPLACABLE EXPRESSION AS HE resurrected painful memories of his little daughter's death. It was all very well for ministers to preach submission to God's will, but what about Elizabeth Clawson's role in bringing about his child's untimely end? Whatever God's ultimate motives in allowing this to happen, John Finch was convinced that a witch had murdered his daughter. He wanted revenge.

"I've been thinking about the quarrel my wife and I had with Goody Clawson a year ago," he declared to Mary Newman, "and the price we paid for crossing her. It was soon after that quarrel that our daughter was taken with screaming and crying—the poor child was in agony. I remember well the night that it began. We opened her clothing and examined her body, but found nothing that might be causing her such pain and suffering. She continued in anguish for about a fortnight and then she died. We were sure that Goody Clawson had a hand in it."

As Goodman Finch was relating this chain of events to Goody Newman in the street outside her house, Thomas Penoir and his wife, Lydia, joined them. After greeting their neighbors, the Penoirs listened intently as the conversation continued.

"About two years past," confided Goody Newman, "I also had a difference with Goody Clawson and angry words passed between us. The next day we had three sheep die suddenly. When we opened them up we couldn't find anything amiss to explain their deaths. Some of our neighbors told us then they thought the creatures were bewitched." Goodwife Penoir nodded. "I remember you telling me about that. Goody Clawson was angry because your daughter had taken some fruit from her orchard." "That's right," said Goody Newman. "She told me at the time, 'If you allow your children to steal when they are young, what will they be like when they grow up?' Do you recall that?" "I do," said Goody Penoir, "and I'm ready to swear to it."

As news of Katherine Branch's accusations against Elizabeth Clawson spread through Stamford's tightly knit community, the Wescots were not alone in recalling past disagreements with Goody Clawson and the afflictions that followed. Nor would this be the first time that Stamford residents explained mysterious ailments in terms of grudges between neighbors and even within families. Older townsfolk remembered well the curmudgeonly William Graves. Some thirty years before, Goodman Graves had refused to hand over his daughter Abigail's inheritance, as he had promised, on her marriage to Samuel Dibble. The angry young husband brought a lawsuit against his father-in-law. Goodman

Graves denied having made the promise and told his son-in-law that he would regret the lawsuit as long as he lived.

"Now do not threaten, father," Samuel replied, "for threatened folk live long."

"Well you shall never live the longer for it," declared Goodman Graves with a scowl.

Abigail tried to persuade her husband to be more "yielding," as she put it. "You do not know," she warned, "what he can do to us."

"I fear no man," Samuel Dibble retorted—rashly as it turned out.

What followed became town legend. Abigail was pregnant and about a fortnight before she was due to give birth, William Graves paid his daughter a visit. "Abigail," he declared, "fit thyself to meet the Lord. For if you are not delivered of the child quickly, I believe you will die."

Several neighbors who were present saw the look of consternation that Abigail gave her husband on hearing her father's grim warning. There followed a long and exceptionally difficult labor during which Abigail suffered much trembling and claimed to be bitten all over. The midwives in attendance shook their heads and muttered that this was no ordinary childbirth. The young couple feared that Abigail was bewitched and that her father was responsible.

William Graves agreed that his daughter was under an evil hand, but denied that he was the culprit. He declared that if Abigail died he would want everyone in the town to come and lay hands on her body: when the murderer touched her corpse, the body would move and so expose the miscreant. There was general relief in Stamford when Abigail gave birth successfully and survived, not only for her sake and the child's: the prospect of a postmortem investigation with Goodman Graves watching closely as his neighbors lined up to lay hands on his daughter's corpse sent shivers down many a spine. Soon afterward local magistrates conducted an inquiry into allegations that William Graves had bewitched his daughter, but they concluded that there was insufficient evidence to prosecute.

As fear of witchcraft again cast its shadow over Stamford, the allegations this time came from not one but many households. Once Katherine Branch named her tormentors, beginning with Elizabeth Clawson, townspeople gathered in knots of righteous anxiety to relive their many ugly encounters with Goody Clawson and to vent their long-festering suspicions against her.

It made good sense to folk such as John Finch, Mary Newman, and Thomas and Lydia Penoir that they should explain their misfortunes in terms of bewitchment by vengeful neighbors. Much that occurred in their lives was mysterious and unnerving: physicians and midwives were all too often perplexed by their neighbors' ailments; loved ones, livestock, and crops frequently sickened for no apparent reason. But such adversities were incomprehensible only until one looked beyond the natural realm. In common with other New England settlers, the people of Stamford believed that supernatural forces intruded constantly into their lives. The Reverend Bishop taught that all adversities were sent by the Almighty to punish sinners, warn of His anger, and test faith through adversity. Whosoever inflicted the harm, it should be understood as God's will. But some of the pastor's flock were more inclined in times of affliction to seek out the more immediate and human causes of their problems. The people of Stamford did not need a minister to teach them that just beyond the range of the eye there glimmered a realm of occult forces that, if harnessed by malevolent folk, could inflict grievous harm. Personal experience and shocking stories that passed from household to household, from community to community, from one side of the Atlantic to the other, and from generation to generation taught that enemies in their midst could wield dark skills with ghastly results.

Enmities tended to be intense and festering in communities such as Stamford, for the simple reason that everyone's welfare depended on personal cooperation. Day-to-day life involved innumerable informal exchanges and favors between neighbors, relatives, friends, and sometimes enemies. Mary Newman would have obtained most of the household goods that she did not produce herself from her neighbors: perhaps she had exchanged some of the soap she recently made for a dozen of Goodwife Penoir's candles. Thomas Penoir may have been about to ask several neighbors for help as he put up a new barn, just as over the years he had helped them when they needed extra hands or went through hard times. No doubt he could talk with them when they met at the next town meeting, or perhaps before then at the local tavern.

Stamford's minister taught that mutual assistance was a spiritual as well as practical necessity. Brothers and sisters in Christ should be knit together not only by day-to-day needs but also by godly affection and their common religious quest. Theirs was first and foremost a community of souls, the Reverend Bishop declared. The people of Stamford should reinforce each other's faith, watch over each other in mutual stewardship, and rein each other in when temptation seemed to be luring them into sin.

That emphasis on community support created intense pressure. When requests for help were denied and when neighbors argued, resentments and recriminations often lingered. People knew that conflict threatened to undermine the values on which their community was built: discord was, as the Reverend Bishop often reminded them, an opening to the Devil, who was always looking for ways to poison the well of God's vineyard. No one wanted to be held responsible for that happening.

Those who refused a neighbor's request or quarreled with other townsfolk often felt guilty about their behavior. Some would look inward, examine their consciences, and try to mend their ways. Others preferred to focus on the anger of those they had wronged: they would watch for any misfortune that could be laid at the aggrieved party's door and then conclude that they were the victims of a neighbor's vengeful temper. Goody Clawson acted as if she was the injured party when the Newmans' daughter stole from her orchard, but the Newmans saw things differently. When they found three sheep inexplicably dead the very next day, their quarrel with Goody Clawson and the ever-present threat of occult attack coalesced to provide a logical explanation for their misfortune—witchcraft.

Similar resentments and suspicions swirled around Mercy Disborough as the residents of Compo recalled disputes with their sharp-tongued neighbor and the misfortunes that ensued. About a year ago, thirty-nine-year-old Henry Grey recalled, one of his calves had began to act very strangely, running around in distress as if trying to escape from something and roaring in the oddest way for six or seven hours at a time. A lamb had also sickened without warning and died within the hour. When they skinned it, the creature looked as if it had been bruised or pinched on the shoulders, something he had never seen before. Then, in the spring of 1692, one of Goodman Grey's cows drowned in a swamp. Soon afterward another suddenly weakened for no apparent reason, refused to eat, and collapsed.

Henry Grey had quarreled on several occasions with the Disboroughs and suspected that Goody Disborough was bewitching his livestock. She had told Goodman Grey's neighbors Thomas and Elizabeth Benit that she could not abide him ever since he received some apples from her mother and claimed that they weighed less than she told him. That was eighteen years ago. More recently, in early 1692, Henry Grey's relationship with the Disboroughs had taken a turn for the worse. He needed a kettle and bargained for one with the Disboroughs. It seemed new when he first saw it, with fresh hammer strokes clearly visible on the metal surface. But within minutes of returning home with it, the kettle changed its appearance; it now looked old and battered, with several punctures that had been filled in with nails. Goodman Grey returned it, which did not please the Disboroughs. Goody Disborough was especially angry and many hard words passed between them. It was after that confrontation that one of Goodman Grey's cows drowned and another collapsed.

Thomas Benit was not in the least surprised when he heard about this sequence of events. "Do you recall," asked Benit, turn-

This drawing of English witch suspect Jennet Dibble captures effectively the stereotype of the witch as a willful, crabby, and unforgiving older woman. (SOURCE: DRAWING IN IN-DIA INK FROM "A DISCOURSE OF WITCHCRAFT" BY EDWARD FAIRFAX, WRITTEN BETWEEN 1621 AND 1623, COURTESY OF THE BRITISH LIBRARY.)

ing to his wife, "when Mercy Disborough told me she'd make me as bare as a bird's tail? That was two or three years ago, just before our livestock began to die. Soon afterward I found two calves in the creek, both dead. A fortnight later I lost full thirty lambs, all doing well till then, and not long after that another two calves—they seemed well enough when I last looked in on them at night and yet they were dead the next morning."

Elizabeth Benit nodded, recalling the hardship that losing so many livestock had caused them. Mercy Disborough could not be made to pay for the animals, but now perhaps a different kind of justice would be meted out by the magistrates. "Remember, husband, what daughter Elizabeth told us two summers ago."

Goodman Benit remembered well. Their daughter had ac-companied Ann Godfrey, perhaps foolishly, to see how Goody Disborough would react on being told that neighbors suspected her of witchcraft. "Henry Grey's wife thinks you bewitched their oxen," Goody Godfrey told Disborough, "and that you made four of them jump over the fence. She also says you bewitched their beer, so that it burst out of the barrel."

Mercy Disborough was not pleased. She began to vent bitterly about the rumors and allegations that her neighbors were spreading. "A woman came to my house recently," she complained, "when I was in the midst of devotion. She reviled me and asked what I was doing. 'Praying to my God,' I said. Then she asked me who my God was and told me my God was the Devil. I bade her get out and go home to pray to her God. I know not if she did pray or not, but God met with her. She died a hard death for reviling me."

After they took leave of Goody Disborough the two young women returned to the Benits' home, where Elizabeth revealed to Ann Godfrey a crucial fact that neither she nor Goody Disborough had chosen to mention during their exchange.

"The woman Goody Disborough spoke of was my sister and I heard about the words that Goody Disborough said passed between them. She did indeed die a hard death."

"I think that we should go back," said Ann, "and talk with her again."

"Why would you want to do that?" asked Thomas Benit. "You should leave well alone, or Mercy will do you some mischief."

That night Goody Godfrey could not sleep. She heard a strange noise in the house and also a commotion outside, as if an animal were being attacked. The next morning she and her husband found one of their heifers lying dead near the door.

Damaging though these stories were, there was much more besides. Many of Goody Disborough's neighbors had heard that she could sometimes be persuaded to unbewitch her victims, clear proof of occult powers. In the late 1680s, one of John Grumman's children had suddenly sickened; neither he nor his wife could tell what was wrong. They suspected foul play. John Grumman's nephew, Thomas Benit, Jr., told him that he should visit Goodwife Disborough. After all, anyone with any sense could tell that she was a witch.

Goodman Grumman was well aware that the Benits had quarreled with Goody Disborough. Because he and the Benits were related, she might be taking revenge by harming his child. But he flatly refused to confront her, explaining to his nephew that doing so might make the situation worse. Young Benit decided to take matters into his own hands. He strode over to Mercy Disborough's house and told her without ceremony to come and unbewitch his uncle's child. "Or else," he declared, "I'll tear your heart out."

Goody Disborough replied in astonishment that she had no idea what he was talking about. She accompanied Thomas Benit back to his uncle's house, where she examined and stroked the sick child with what looked like genuine concern. "God forbid I should hurt the child," she declared, shaking her head, and departed with a reproachful glance at her accusers. From anyone else such a display of concern would have been welcome and touching, but neither the Grummans nor the Benits trusted Goody Disborough. That distrust deepened when the child's condition improved within a few hours. Such a speedy recovery seemed highly suspicious.

Ann Godfrey had a similar experience. Goody Disborough had made no secret of her resentment after her encounter with Ann and Elizabeth Benit. Goody Godfrey feared that the death of her heifer would not be the end of the quarrel, and when another of their sows fell sick the following summer, she knew instinctively that Goody Disborough's evil eye was at work again. As the witch passed by her house, Ann Godfrey called out. "Come over here, Goody Disborough! I know you've bewitched my household before and now you do it again. There are folks who talk of making you pay for your witchcraft. Unbewitch my sow or you'll regret it." Goodwife Disborough scowled at her and continued on her way without even responding. But soon after that the sow recovered.

Such stories, accumulating year after year and passed on from neighbor to neighbor, boded ill for Mercy Disborough. In addition to suspected bewitchments, other strange and surely supernatural incidents intensified fears that Goody Disborough was a witch. In September 1692, when the special court convened in Fairfield, twenty-nine-year-old Edward Jesop made the short journey from Compo to relate what had happened when he visited the Disboroughs' house late one day the previous winter.

"Thomas Disborough asked me to stay for dinner," Edward declared. "I could see that a pig was roasting and it looked very fine, so I accepted with thanks. But when Goody Disborough brought the pig to table, it seemed to have no skin and looked very odd. We had plenty of light, so I'm sure I was not mistaken. Yet when Thomas began to slice the pig, the skin seemed to have reappeared and the pig looked exactly as it had on the spit, at which strange alteration I was much concerned. But fearing to displease Goody Disborough, I did accept some of the pig.

"That same evening Isaac Sherwood was also there and debated a piece of scripture with Goody Disborough. I being of the same mind as him concerning the passage and Sherwood telling her where the passage was, Goody Disborough got out a Bible so as to read the text. The Bible had large print and the light was good, but though I looked earnestly at the page I could not see one letter. Yet looking at it again when Goody Disborough turned over a few leaves, I could see and read it from over a yard away.

"Later that night," Edward continued, "on the way home, I reached Compo Creek and the water seemed high, so I went to fetch a canoe on the bank about fifty yards away. Ordinarily I can shove it into the creek with ease, but though I lifted with all my might and managed to get one end up from the ground, I could by no means push it into the creek. I then noticed that the water seemed to be low enough that I could ride across after all, but by the time that I got on my horse and rode back to the bank the water appeared to be as high as before. I returned to the canoe and again could not budge it, so decided to ride around the creek. I'd gone that way many times and know it as well as the road in front of my house. I had my old cart horse Joe with me and you know how steady he is. But I couldn't keep him in the road, no matter what I did. He kept turning off the road into the bushes or backing up nervously. We kept losing our way and wandered for most of the night before we managed to get home, though it was not much more than two miles."

It is highly unlikely that Mercy Disborough's trial was the first occasion on which Edward Jesop told this story. We can imagine him confiding in neighbors, perhaps at the tavern one evening—and they, glancing at one another as he paused in mid-tale to take a swig from a mug of beer, a few with barely concealed amusement and incredulity, but others clearly unnerved by what they were hearing. None of what Edward said could have completely surprised those listening, given what they had heard over the years about Mercy Disborough. Vague fears and suspicion now coalesced into firmer conviction that their neighbor was using dark powers to confound the residents of Compo. If they were right, no one was safe while Mercy Disborough remained at liberty.

Yet Goody Disborough's neighbors were not defenseless against her occult machinations. When Henry Grey began to suspect she was bewitching his livestock, he decided to try an experiment that would, if he got it right, undo the damage she had inflicted and injure her in return. Goodman Grey had heard that boiling the blood or urine of a bewitched person, heating the hair or fingernail clippings of the victim over a fire, burning a bewitched object, or inflicting an injury upon a bewitched animal would put an end to the witchcraft and translate the harm back onto the witch. The witch would be hurt and exposed by the sudden injury—an antidote and revenge!

New England ministers urged their flocks to refrain from such experiments, declaring that these were not ordained by God in holy scripture and so must depend on the Devil's assistance. No good person, they declared, would go to the Devil for help against the Devil. God would expose the witch if and when He saw fit. Meanwhile, the victim should pray and repent for sins that may have played a role in prompting the affliction. But some folk quietly ignored such strictures. If a witch was involved in their troubles, they wanted to strike back. And how could it be that the use of defensive magic against a witch was itself evil?

Goodman Grey recalled hearing that Elizabeth Seager, a Hartford woman accused of witchcraft in the 1660s, was identified and punished in this way. One of Elizabeth Seager's neighbors, Goodwife Garrett, had taken a cheese out of storage to find one side full of maggots and the other completely unharmed. Goodwife Garrett suspected that Goody Seager had bewitched the cheese. Elizabeth Seager happened to be in their barn husking corn and so Goody Garrett flung the maggoty side into the fire. Immediately, she heard Goodwife Seager cry out and shortly afterward she came into the house, complaining of terrible pains: "What do I ail? What do I ail?"

Goodwife Garrett and her husband recounted that incident in court when Elizabeth Seager was tried for witchcraft. Henry Grey did not know (and nor do we) how that evidence figured in the jury's deliberations, but perhaps he could produce similar evidence against Goody Disborough. Accordingly, he cut off a piece of the sick heifer's ear, hoping that would do the trick. But the animal remained almost lifeless. Goodman Grey then sent for his cart whip and struck the cow with it. She immediately clambered to her feet and ran away. Henry Grey followed and struck her several times. Within an hour, the heifer had recovered completely and chewed her cud quite contentedly.

There was now no doubt in Goodman Grey's mind that someone had cast an evil eye on his cattle. Flogging the cow had undone the spell and its injury would be translated back onto the witch. Grey asked his neighbors to let him know if they saw any-one in the town suffering from unusual pains. The following day he received a report from Ann Godfrey. She told him that she had just been to visit Thomas and Mercy Disborough. Goody Disborough was lying prostrate on her bed. She stretched out her arm to Ann and declared piteously, "I am almost killed."

A few weeks later, Henry Grey met Goody Disborough un-expectedly at his brother Jacob's house. She was still harping on their disagreement over the kettle and made no effort to hide her pleasure over his recent problems.

"I said when you wouldn't keep the kettle that it would cost you two cows." Her self-righteous tone infuriated Goodman Grey, but it also occurred to him that she had made a serious tactical error.

"I can prove you said that," he retorted.

"Aye," she said in a quite different tone of voice and then fell silent.

On returning home, Goodman Grey's wife informed him that one of their calves had suddenly taken sick that day and so she had sent for their whip, but the calf was back on its feet by the time that the whip arrived. So far as Henry Grey could tell, the incident had taken place about the same time as his confronta-tion with Goody Disborough.

Now Goodman Grey heard that magistrates had arrested Goody Disborough and were questioning her about the torments of a young woman in nearby Stamford. The magistrates appar-ently wanted to hear from anyone with information bearing on their investigation. This was his opportunity. Henry Grey arranged to meet with a court official in Fairfield to record his testimony. He took Ann Godfrey with him so that she could repeat her account of Mercy Disborough's prostration.

Meanwhile, similar experiments were taking place within the Wescots' household. Some of the neighbors watching over Kate decided to cut off a lock of her hair to burn it and perhaps bring her relief. If one of the women Kate had named was seen with a burn over the next few days, that would confirm that she was the witch responsible. Kate was in one of her trances when this was under discussion and did not seem to be aware of what was going on around her. Yet each time one of the neighbors approached with scissors, she drew back quickly. Even when they tried to cut Kate's hair from behind, creeping up on her quietly and without warning, she would immediately turn around and prevent it. The witch afflicting her was evidently anxious to prevent them from carrying out the experiment.

After several failed attempts, one of the men present took Kate in his arms to restrain her forcibly so that a lock of her hair could be cut. Kate was a frail slip of a girl, yet she now became so strong and seemingly so heavy that he could not hold her still. The others in the room still could not get at her hair. Kate cried out as if she were in agony and eventually they gave up.

When Kate came to herself, they asked her if she would now be willing to have a lock of her hair cut off. "Yes," she replied, "you can have all of it if you like." Here was compelling proof, her watchers agreed, that Kate was bewitched. Between her fits she was eager to cooperate, hoping to end her ordeal, but when controlled by the witches she would not, or could not, allow anything to be done that might incriminate the women afflicting her.

There were those in Stamford who believed that Kate had re-sisted being bled by the midwife Goody Bates for the same rea-son. Mistress Wescot wanted her servant bled because at the time she was not certain whether Kate's fits were caused by disease or supernatural assault. Kate, who had been lying in a stupor, sud-denly leapt to life as the midwife prepared to operate. Some neighbors suspected that Kate's fits were counterfeit and she sim-ply did not want to be cut, but others wondered if the witches had caused her to resist—perhaps her tormentors were afraid that if Kate was bled they would be exposed if someone noticed soon afterward that they were also cut.

As a growing number of suspicious incidents came to light, each in turn fueled local fear and hostility toward Goody Claw-son and Goody Disborough. The doubts that some folk had about Kate's credibility had by no means disappeared, but these were increasingly overshadowed by the accumulation of evidence against the accused. For years people had shared their suspicions only with trusted friends and relatives. After all, courts were of-ten fickle in dealing with witchcraft cases: they would ask for in-formation against an accused person and then, like as not, judge it inadequate, so that the witches went free. Goodwife Seager, ex-posed through the burning of maggoty cheese, had been con-victed in 1665 but released the following year when the gover-nor's council rejected the grounds on which the jury had found her guilty. Accusing someone of witchcraft was risky because witches were notoriously vengeful and if set free might well wreak havoc among those who had testified against them. But once

Daniel Wescot stepped forward, others took heart and volunteered incriminating information against the accused.

As officials gathered evidence throughout the summer, there emerged a long history of suspicion and resentment surrounding the two women. Katherine Branch's allegations against Mercy Disborough and Elizabeth Clawson were clearly part of a larger story. But how would the special court react to such testimony? Would these magistrates prove any more reliable than those who presided over witchcraft cases in the past? Surely the overwhelming volume of evidence against the two women would force the court to act decisively. Such was its duty as protector of the peace and of the King and Queen's subjects. Such, at least, were the hopes of those who believed the accused to be guilty as charged.

· *Five* ·

WEIGHING THE EVIDENCE

W ILLIAM JONES, CONNECTICUT'S DEPUTY-GOVERNOR AND A member of the special court appointed to deal with the witch accusations in Stamford and Compo, did not take his responsibilities lightly. There survives in the archives a memorandum in William Jones's handwriting that summarizes carefully the established procedures for prosecuting an accused witch. It includes two sets of requirements: one for arresting and examining someone suspected of witchcraft, the other for convicting and hanging an indicted witch. Mister Jones most likely compiled this guide in preparation for the trials that would take place at the end of the summer in Fairfield. Like most other New England magistrates, William Jones had no legal training; he sat on the bench as a part-time public service, not as a full-time professional career. But he had devoted considerable time and energy to reading legal manuals and theological works that discussed the issues involved in witchcraft cases. He would now presumably compare the requirements for examination and conviction outlined in these texts with the evidence against Elizabeth Clawson and Mercy Disborough.

Presiding over any case that carried the death penalty was a daunting responsibility. New England courts insisted on judicial rigor in capital cases: they demanded clear proof of guilt and required two independent witnesses for each incriminating act. In many cases where the evidence was circumstantial or problematic in some other way, magistrates handed down a sentence short of death, even as they voiced their suspicion that the defendant was, in fact, guilty. Some of the crimes that carried the death penalty were extremely difficult to prove beyond reasonable doubt—and none more so than witchcraft, a supernatural and therefore invisible crime. If a defendant was willing to confess, the problem disappeared. In 1663 Rebecca Greensmith from Hartford, Connecticut, went to the gallows after admitting that she had signed a compact with the Devil and used witchcraft to harm her enemies. But confessions were rare and without them magistrates were left with evidence that was mostly either circumstantial or spectral. Most magistrates considered the former a dubious basis on which to justify a death sentence and, as for the latter, could one trust information given by specters, which were, after all, the emissaries of the Devil?

Courts charged with the handling of witchcraft cases had to deal not only with strict legal requirements but also with public opinion. Few ordinary folk appreciated the rigorous standards of proof that judges were bound to uphold: they often considered the evidence presented in court to be clearly damning and felt betrayed if the accused was acquitted. The most infamous clash between the legal system and public opinion in Connecticut had been some thirty years before, when Elizabeth Seager was tried for witchcraft on three separate occasions and each time went free: the first and second of these trials, both of which took place in 1663, resulted in acquittal; at the third trial in 1665 a jury did convict her, but the Court of Assistants overturned the verdict. Magistrates sometimes tried to contain public anger by recognizing quite openly in their formal judgments that legal innocence did not necessarily mean actual innocence. In one case they found the accused "suspiciously guilty of witchcraft, but not legally guilty according to law and evidence received." In another they judged the defendant to be "not legally guilty according to indictment," but acknowledged "just ground of vehement suspicion" against her.

Magistrates wanted New Englanders to believe that courts charged with witchcraft cases took seriously the testimony that accusers submitted, even though that testimony could not always support a conviction. At the close of yet another trial the judges advised the defendant "solemnly to reflect upon the case and grounds of suspicion given in and alleged against her," and told her that "if further grounds of suspicion of witchcraft or fuller evidences should appear against her by reason of mischief done to the bodies or estate of any by any preternatural acts proved against her, she might justly fear and expect to be brought to her trial for it." Elizabeth Seager's experience suggested that the neighbors of suspect witches, if not the suspects themselves, took such advice to heart.

The cases of Elizabeth Clawson and Mercy Disborough would test the judicial and diplomatic skills of William Jones and his fellow magistrates to their utmost limits. Mister Jones came to Fairfield fully prepared, having read extensively on the vexed issue of how to conduct a witch trial. Most of the texts he examined had been published in England, including William Perkins's famous *Discourse on the Damned Art of Witchcraft* and Richard Bernard's no less respected *Guide to Grand-Jury Men*. Both authors wanted to establish a straightforward and reliable procedure for trying witches; he had found their careful discussion of the issues involved invaluable. Increase Mather, a learned pastor who lived in Boston, had penned his own contribution to the scholarship, an *Essay for the Recording of Illustrious Providences*. Published in 1684, this was a fount of wisdom on the subject of witchcraft as well as other supernatural phenomena. William Jones summarized the information that he gleaned from these various authorities in notes that would guide him as he assessed the evidence against Elizabeth Clawson and Mercy Disborough. Thus armed, he hoped to play a creditable role in the court's proceedings as it sought to juggle its twin roles as an instrument of God against the forces of darkness and a rigorous agent of the law.

Mister Jones's memorandum was divided into two parts. The first gave a list of legitimate grounds for holding a formal inquiry following an accusation of witchcraft. According to the authors he had read, officials should launch an investigation if any one of the following conditions was met:

Grounds for Examination of a Witch

1. Notorious defamation by the common report of the people a ground of suspicion.
2. A second ground for strict examination is if a fellow witch gives testimony on his examination or death that such a person is a witch. But this is not sufficient for conviction or condemnation.

3. If after cursing there follows death or at least mischief to the party.

4. If after quarreling or threatening a person mischief doth follow, for parties devilishly disposed after cursings do use threatenings and that also is a great presumption against them.

5. If the party suspected be the son or daughter, the servant or familiar friend, near neighbor or old companion of a known or convicted witch, this also a presumption, for witchcraft is an art that may be learned and conveyed from man to man and oft it falleth out that a witch dying leaveth some of the aforesaid heirs of her witchcraft.

6. If the party suspected have the Devil's mark, for 'tis thought when the Devil maketh his covenant with them he always leaves his mark behind him to know them for his own, that is, if no evident reason in them can be given for such a mark.

7. Lastly, if the party examined be unconstant and contrary to himself in his answers.

It must have been clear to Mister Jones that the local magistrates had acted properly when, based on the information available to them, they held a preliminary hearing and then detained the suspects. This was true even of Mary Staples, Mary Harvey, and Hannah Harvey. Goodwife Staples had long been associated by "common report" with witchcraft and so satisfied the first of the "grounds" itemized in the memorandum. Mary Harvey and Hannah Harvey, daughter and grand-daughter of Goody Staples, fulfilled another, the fifth, by being closely related to Goody Staples.

The depositions against both Goody Clawson and Goody Disborough satisfied several of William Jones's criteria, most obviously the first and fourth, "the common report of the people" and "mischief" following "quarreling or threatening." Neighbors in Compo and Stamford had long suspected the two women of witchcraft; a significant number had, moreover, suffered death or misfortune within their households after quarreling with one of the accused.

Goody Disborough had also cursed at least two of her neighbors, which satisfied the third ground for examination. Following a disagreement with Elizabeth Benit, she informed the young woman rather cryptically "that it should be pressed, heaped, and running over to her." When Elizabeth Benit reacted with outrage to this malediction, Mercy Disborough responded that the words she had spoken were taken from scripture. But she also told Elizabeth Benit's father-in-law, Thomas Benit, that "she would make him as bare as a bird's tail." Soon after that his livestock began to die under mysterious circumstances.

In addition, both Elizabeth Clawson and Mercy Disborough satisfied the sixth of the possible grounds for an inquiry: both were rumored to have a "Devil's mark" or "witch's teat" on their bodies, an abnormal lump of flesh that looked like an extra nipple. Demonic imps were said to drink blood from these witch teats, usually assuming animal form to do so. Katherine Branch claimed to have seen Goody Miller, the suspect who escaped to New York, feeding a dog from a teat under her arm.

Several women in Stamford who had cared for Elizabeth Clawson during childbirth came forward in June 1692 to testify that she had a physical abnormality, perhaps a Devil's mark. But not everyone agreed that Goody Clawson differed from other women "in the make of her body." The court of inquiry had appointed a group of women, "faithfully sworn, narrowly and truly to inspect and search her body, to see whether any suspicious signs or marks did appear that were not common or that were preternatural." These women reported "with one voice" that "they found nothing save a wart on one of her arms." They also searched Mercy Disborough's body that same day and did find "a teat or something like one in her privy parts, at least an inch long, which is not common in other women, and for which they could give no natural reason."

Once Elizabeth Clawson and Mercy Disborough had been detained and removed to Fairfield, the group of women reconvened to carry out a second search of both women's bodies. The local magistrates were clearly worried about the inconsistencies in what they had heard so far. The women confirmed that there was "nothing" on Goody Clawson's body "that is not common to other women." On Goody Disborough's body they found "as before and nothing else."

According to the guidelines on which William Jones was relying, the discovery of an unusual mark justified proceeding against a suspect "if no evident reason can be given for such a mark." Yet it was easier said than done to establish whether a marking or growth was natural or supernatural. Mister Jones may well have seen the trial records for a case from several decades earlier in which residents of Fairfield disagreed over whether marks found on a woman named Goodwife Knapp, executed as a witch, were really witch teats. After Goody Knapp was cut down and brought to be buried, Mary Staples (the very same woman now accused by Katherine Branch) examined her body.

"Here are no more teats than I myself have, or any other women, or you either if you would search your body," she told one of the other women present.

"I know not what you have," the woman replied, "but for myself, if any find such things about me, I deserve to be hanged as she was."

Several other women could not at first find any suspicious markings on Goody Knapp, but changed their minds under pressure from those who believed they had seen the Devil's mark. Even Goody Staples ended up admitting that the marks might well be teats and that "no honest women had such."

William Jones and his colleagues now arranged for a group of women, including some of those who had examined the accused before and others who had not yet seen their bodies, to carry out a third examination. Sarah Gold and Ann Wakeman, testifying on behalf of this group, gave a somewhat different report from those submitted earlier in the summer: "concerning Goody Clawson, we find in her private parts more than is common to women, we can't say teats, but something extraordinary, and Goody Disborough's is something like it, but a great deal smaller. Goody Clawson's is a dark red and Disborough's of a pale color." Yet Goody Gold and Goody Wakeman did not speak for all of the women, as Ann Hardy and Martha Henry made clear in their separate deposition: "naught is seen by us on the body of Elizabeth Clawson which we could not find before at Stamford and on Mercy's body we find that what we saw on her before is grown somewhat less, but there's now another small one which we saw not before."

Other women now came forward to clarify what they had seen at the original examination in Stamford: Sarah Finch, Mary Ambler, and Bethia Weld declared "that they found nothing upon the said Clawson but what they thought was natural, yet do further say that the said Clawson did differ in the make of her body from themselves." Martha Homes confirmed "what return she made unto the court concerning the said search, that at Stamford they found nothing upon the said Clawson but what she thought was natural, yet also doth say that the said Clawson did differ from other women, and that at Fairfield there was then more to be seen upon her than she saw when she was searched at Stamford."

There was clearly no consensus among the women who had examined the defendants' bodies as to what they saw or what it meant. Regardless of whether the marks were natural or not, the magistrates already had ample grounds on which to proceed. But Mister Jones and his colleagues had good reason for their preoccupation with this particular kind of evidence: if truly diabolical, the markings constituted hard physical evidence, which was all too often elusive in a witchcraft trial. As the deputy-governor reviewed the second half of his memorandum, listing the legitimate grounds for conviction, he must have become increasingly concerned that, without proof of the Devil's mark, convicting either woman seemed unlikely. They might well be guilty, but proving that in a court of law was not going to be easy.

The second part of the guide Mister Jones had compiled evaluated various kinds of evidence that might be presented once a witchcraft case came to trial. Legal experts and theologians had recently devoted much ink to distinguishing between "proofs" that they considered "sufficient" for conviction and those they dismissed as inadequate. Three main categories of evidence were judged to be "insufficient":

> 1. Less sufficient are those used in former ages such as by red-hot iron and scalding water, the party to put his hand in one or take up the other. If not hurt the party cleared, if hurt convicted for a witch. But this way utterly condemned in some countries. Another proof justified by some of the learned is by casting the party bound into water. If she sinks counted innocent, if she sink not then guilty.

No one involved in this investigation was suggesting that Elizabeth Clawson or Mercy Disborough put her hand in scalding water or pick up a red-hot iron. But the water test—or ducking, as some called it—was quite another matter. Ducking involved binding suspects and then throwing them into water to see if they sank or not. If they floated, the water had rejected their bodies as unholy and so they were guilty; if they sank, they were innocent.

Daniel Wescot told the court that when he confronted Goody Clawson that May about the afflictions in his household, he asked if she would be willing to be ducked. Elizabeth Clawson replied that she would if the minister and magistrates said it was reliable, but otherwise not. Immediately after Goody Disborough's removal from the court of inquiry in Stamford to the county jail in Fairfield, she actually requested to be ducked and was evidently eager for this to be done. When the jailer asked why, she responded that "it was to vindicate her innocency."

A TRIAL BY WATER *The experiment is being watched by three gentlemen on the river bank; a young man observes from the roof of a nearby watermill. In the background a cart wheel has broken, scattering sacks of grain, perhaps because the driver was distracted by the water trial. It is not clear whether the hog on the riverbank is eyeing one of the sacks or the witch suspect's ordeal—perhaps both. Meanwhile two other hogs are swimming in the river, much to the consternation of a man who is floating rather precariously in a barrel, presumably to observe the experiment at close quarters and to assist the woman if she sinks and so proves her innocence.* (SOURCE: FROM *WITCHES APPREHENDED, EXAMINED AND EXECUTED* [LONDON, 1613]. THIS ITEM IS REPRODUCED BY KIND PERMISSION OF THE HUNTINGTON LIBRARY, SAN MARINO, CALIFORNIA.)

We do not know if John Bishop, the minister at Stamford, did approve of ducking, but officials at Fairfield complied with Mercy Disborough's request. On 2 June both women were bound hand and foot and then thrown into the water. According to those present, Elizabeth Clawson bobbed up and down like a cork and when they tried to push her down she immediately buoyed up again. Mercy Disborough also failed to sink. If the test was trustworthy, both women were guilty.

But William Jones knew from his reading that this technique, though practiced for centuries, was now extremely controversial. Increase Mather addressed the issue in his *Essay for the Recording of Illustrious Providences*. The minister acknowledged that some educated authors defended ducking, their justification being, as William Jones paraphrased it, that "the witch, having made a compact with the Devil, hath renounced her baptism, hence the antipathy between her and water." But Increase Mather rejected this line of reasoning. "All water is not the water of baptism," he wrote, "only that which is used in the very act of baptism." There was, he explained, no natural explanation for witches' bodies being more inclined to float: "The bodies of witches have not lost their natural properties; they have weight in them as much as others. Moral changes and viciousness of mind make no alteration as to these natural properties which are inseparable from the body." If the experiment worked it must be because either God or the Devil had intervened. Since the Bible made no mention of any such technique having been ordained by God, ducking must be an invention of the Devil. And, as Increase Mather pointed out, there was no reason to trust that the

Father of Lies was providing reliable information. "The matter is ultimately resolved into a diabolical faith. And shall that cast the scale, when the lives of men are concerned? Suppose the Devil saith these persons are witches, must the judge therefore condemn them?" Such practices, he declared, were akin to witchcraft itself, relying as they did on a diabolical agency.

Equally problematic, the deputy-governor's notes suggested, were claims by afflicted persons that they had seen images of the witches who caused their torments:

> 2. Another insufficient testimony of a witch is the testimony of a wizard who pretends to show the face of the witch to the party afflicted in a glass. But this he counts diabolical and dangerous. The Devil may represent a person innocent.

Sometimes local "cunning folk" who claimed to have powers of divination were asked by their neighbors to help identify who was causing the bewitchment. But theologians warned that God had not granted such powers to mankind, so that even seemingly benign "cunning" must come from the Devil. If diabolical, it could not be trusted: as Mister Jones wrote in his notes, "the Devil may represent an innocent person."

No one had reported using "cunning" of this sort to expose the witches in Stamford and Compo. But Katherine Branch's testimony about specters that she claimed to have seen during her fits and the information these specters gave her could be placed in the same category. Even if Kate herself could be trusted, which some doubted, these revelations came not from God but the Devil. How could such evidence be trusted? Mister Jones and his colleagues were well aware that the trials taking place further north in Massachusetts were under attack precisely because of their reliance on spectral testimony. In June 1692 twelve ministers had submitted to the Massachusetts governor and his council a joint statement of which William Jones may have seen a copy. The clergymen rejected spectral evidence as a sound basis even for committing suspects, let alone convicting them, because it was "received only on the Devil's authority." An anonymous pamphlet printed in Philadelphia a few months later made a similar point: "What credit is legally to be given to a thing which a human person swears merely upon the Devil's information?"

Experts also rejected the claim that illness or misfortune following an argument between a suspected witch and her alleged victim provided an adequate basis for conviction:

> 3. If after curses and threats mischief follow or if a sick person likely to die take it on his death that such a one has bewitched him, those are strong grounds of suspicion for strict examination but not sufficient for conviction.

William Jones knew that most of the testimony provided by Stamford and Compo residents related to mishaps that occurred after quarrels with one or other of the accused. He agreed with the legal experts that circumstantial evidence of this kind was hardly firm ground on which to stand when condemning someone to death. Still, it may well have struck him as unfortunate that such evidence was accepted as "strong grounds of suspicion" for a formal inquiry and yet rejected as a proof of conviction: that line of reasoning amounted to raising public expectations that a witch would be held accountable, only then to dash them. Mister Jones could not have looked forward to the challenge of

explaining to those who believed in the guilt of Elizabeth Clawson and Mercy Disborough why most of the testimony against
them was legally "insufficient."

The deputy-governor now shifted his attention to the kinds
of evidence that experts found compelling as a basis for conviction. His memorandum listed in one compact paragraph a series of "sufficient proofs," at least one of which must be satisfied
in order to justify conviction. This list followed closely the guidelines provided by William Perkins and Richard Bernard in their
legal manuals. It was also consistent with Connecticut law and
the procedure followed by courts throughout New England.

> The two proofs sufficient for conviction are either 1st the voluntary
> confession of the party suspected, which is adjudged sufficient proof
> by both divines and lawyers. Or 2nd the testimony of two witnesses
> of good and honest report, avouching one of two things in their
> knowledge before the magistrate, either 1st that the party accused hath
> made a league with the Devil or 2nd hath done some known prac-
> tices of witchcraft. Arguments to prove either must be: if they can
> prove the party hath invoked the Devil for his help (this part of the
> worship the Devil binds witches to); or if the party hath entertained
> a familiar spirit in any form (mouse, cat, or other invisible creature);
> or if they affirm upon oath the party hath done any action or work
> which enforce the compact with the Devil such as to show the face
> of a man in a glass, or used enchantments, or such feats. Divining of
> things to come, raising tempests, or causing the form of a dead man
> to appear, or the like, sufficiently proves a witch.

The list seemed logical enough in the abstract, but as William
Jones related each option to the evidence available against the
two women on trial, his head must have begun to spin.

According to the memorandum, a court should convict only if it had clear proof that the accused was in league with the Devil. Each of New England's capital laws drew on specific biblical passages for their inspiration; the Puritan authorities treated the Bible as a legal as well as devotional guide. Connecticut's law against witchcraft focused on the witch's relationship with "a familiar spirit" appointed by Satan to carry out malevolent deeds on the witch's behalf:

> If any man or woman be a witch, that is, hath or consulteth with a familiar spirit, they shall be put to death. (Exod: 22.18; Lev: 20.27; Deut: 18.10,11.)

The law's wording reflected a theological perspective, treating the crime as a form of heresy in which the offender forsook Christianity, committed to serve the Devil, and in return was allotted a familiar spirit, or demon, to do the witch's bidding. Either the accused must confess to having signed a covenant with the Devil, or there must be at least two reliable witnesses who could testify that the accused had indeed entered a compact with Satan or had inflicted harm through occult means that must involve the Devil's assistance.

Given the religious principles that inspired settlement throughout New England, and the regularity with which ministers reaffirmed those principles in their sermons, one might have expected that the evidence presented in witchcraft cases would be framed in theological terms and so fit well with legal requirements. Yet William Jones was well aware that such had not been the experience of New England magistrates. Most witnesses in witch trials were preoccupied with practical issues. They believed that a neighbor had used occult powers to bring about illness or misfortune and they wanted that neighbor punished. They described in graphic detail their disagreements with the accused and the damage that she subsequently inflicted on them. But few witnesses expressed any interest in where a witch's power came from or her spiritual allegiance; they rarely mentioned the Devil.

Even as most trials ended in acquittal, ordinary folk continued to focus on witchcraft as a practical menace, not as a spiritual betrayal. They may have been motivated partly by stubborn resistance to pressure from the courts, or they may not have understood fully why so many trials were failing to result in conviction. But whatever the reasons, when New Englanders talked about witchcraft, most of them did so in terms of the practical threat that it posed: it seemed at such times that ordinary folk cared not a whit about the Devil, only about their dead sheep.

This was not good news for conscientious magistrates like Mister Jones, who wanted to defend his neighbors against the scourge of witchcraft and yet had to abide by legal standards of proof. Even confessions were now extremely controversial. At the Salem trials, over fifty individuals had confessed to joining a Satanic conspiracy dedicated to overthrowing God's kingdom in New England. But during the summer of 1692 a growing number of these women and men had recanted, claiming that officials had used intimidation and, in some cases, physical torture to extract confessions from them. One man wrote in a petition to five prominent ministers that when his son refused to confess, "they tied him neck and heels till the blood gushed out at his nose, and would have kept him so twenty-four hours, if one more merciful than the rest had not taken pity on him and caused him to be unbound. It is credibly believed and reported that this was the occasion of making others confess what they never did." Some defendants claimed that they confessed in order to save their lives: the court in Salem was staying the execution of those who cooperated with its proceedings; only those who refused to confess and give the names of other witches were hanged.

In light of these embarrassing revelations, if either Goody Clawson or Goody Disborough did confess to witchcraft, the magistrates responsible for their trials would have to take great care that their statements were completely voluntary and seen to be so. But both women insisted when first questioned back in May that they had nothing to do with Katherine Branch's fits and neither showed any sign of confessing to the other bewitchments of which they had been accused since then. Given their obstinacy, the court needed "witnesses of good and honest report" to testify that the accused had "made a league with the Devil" or had "done some known practices of witchcraft."

Yet there was hardly any reliable evidence before the court to suggest that Elizabeth Clawson or Mercy Disborough had conversed with Satan. To be sure, Katherine Branch claimed that the Devil had appeared to her "in the shape of three women, Goody Clawson, Goody Miller, and Goody Disborough." She told the court that Satan wanted her to become a witch and that unless she did so the women who appeared to her in spectral form would kill her. Many people had heard Kate relate what she saw during her fits, yet she was the sole source for all that information and the law required that there be two independent witnesses for each incriminating incident. In any case, the information Kate gave was highly suspect: a significant number of Stamford residents doubted that the young woman's fits were genuine; and even if she was seeing specters, how could anyone be sure that the Devil was not misleading her?

The deputy-governor would also have recalled that earlier that summer Kate had a conversation with the afflicting specters during which she told them that two ministers, John Bishop of Stamford and Thomas Hanford of Norwalk, had recently visited her and warned her not to yield to the Devil. A careful examination of the depositions would have revealed to Mister Jones that Kate did not mention the Devil at all until after the ministers paid her a visit. There were those who suspected that Kate had incriminated Goody Clawson to please her master and mistress. Had she also introduced talk of the Devil into her descriptions so as to accommodate her well-meaning minister? William Jones doubtless appreciated the ministers' efforts to arm Kate against the forces of evil. But as a magistrate he may well have worried that her testimony might not be entirely spontaneous.

Other than Katherine Branch, only one witness had suggested that either of the accused had dealings with the Devil. According to Ann Godfrey, Mercy Disborough told her about a confrontation in which a neighbor "told her that her god was the Devil," an accusation that Mercy had rejected with indignation. Once imprisoned, Goody Disborough claimed that she herself was tormented by the Devil and bewitched. The conversation that Ann Godfrey reported could be seen as legitimate grounds for examination, but on its own it was hardly sufficient to prove that Mercy Disborough was indeed guilty of worshiping Satan.

The suspicious marks that women had found on Goody Disborough's body were much more promising as a sign of the Devil's involvement. Successive examinations had resulted in broadly consistent findings: the markings were "not common in other women" and looked like witch teats; the examiners could find no natural explanation for their presence on her body. The law defined a witch as having a familiar spirit and the deputy-governor's memorandum advised that an accused witch could be convicted if she had "entertained a familiar spirit in any form (mouse, cat, or other invisible creature)." Admittedly, no one had actually seen Mercy Disborough giving suck to an animal familiar. Yet the existence of the witch's teat did suggest that she could and did feed familiar spirits in the same way as Goody Miller, the witch suspect who had fled to New York.

There was one other category of evidence approved as grounds for conviction; namely, "known practices of witchcraft." William Jones's notes defined these as "any action or work which enforce the compact with the Devil, such as to show the face of a man in a glass, enchantments," or "divining of things to come, raising tempests, or causing the form of a dead man to appear." In times of trouble, New Englanders often turned for help to neighbors whom they believed to have occult powers. These men and women were generally valued as "cunning folk" who could tell fortunes, use spells to heal the sick, and defend against occult attack. Many New Englanders saw nothing wrong with the use of such powers for benign ends. But clergymen disagreed. Cunning folk might claim that their powers were harmless and their neighbors might see such skills as a local asset, just so long as they were used to help and not to harm. But in reality, ministers insisted, those powers came from the Devil.

Cunning folk and their occult skills gave rise to much tension between pastors and their flocks. Yet evidence of such activities could prove invaluable to magistrates in a trial for witchcraft. When townsfolk became convinced that one of their neighbors was using "cunning" to harm them and so brought charges of witchcraft against them, they often mentioned in their depositions that the accused had a history of using occult means to tell fortunes or heal the sick—not because they considered these activities objectionable but because they showed that the defendant did indeed have occult powers that were also being used for malicious ends. The legal guidelines on which magistrates such as Mister Jones relied specified that such practices could not work without the Devil's involvement, even if those concerned did not realize it.

Such testimony could be used as grounds for conviction and so was much more helpful to magistrates than a mountain of testimony about misfortunes following quarrels or curses, even though it was the latter that townsfolk routinely produced. When Goodwife Harrison of Wethersfield, Connecticut, was tried for witchcraft in the late 1660s, several witnesses noted that she told fortunes. Local ministers consulted in that case confirmed that "foretelling some future event or revealing of a secret" that could not be "known by human skill" did indicate familiarity with the Devil, insomuch as it communicated knowledge that could only come from Satan. The jury found Goodwife Harrison guilty, but luckily for her the magistrates' insistence on having two witnesses for each incriminating incident led them to overturn the verdict.

Nothing in the depositions that William Jones had before him suggested that either Elizabeth Clawson or Mercy Disborough had a reputation as a cunning woman. Given the absence of testimony that either had carried out "known practices of witchcraft" (other than circumstantial evidence about misfortunes following quarrels with the accused) and given a lack of reliable testimony to show the Devil's involvement, it was difficult to see how the court could justify conviction. Mercy Disborough's bodily markings might possibly count as "sufficient proof," but disagreement about their nature would most likely protect her from conviction on that basis.

At the end of his memorandum, the deputy-governor had written that the servants of Satan were often exposed through "the just judgment of God" and because the Devil's "malice toward all men" drove him to confound even his own disciples. If defendants were convicted of "that horrid crime," they should "be put to death" since "God hath said, 'Thou shalt not suffer a witch to live.' " Yet the authors William Jones had read warned "jurors, etc., not to condemn suspected persons on bare presumptions without good and sufficient proofs." As he considered the evidence presented against Elizabeth Clawson and Mercy Disborough, the problems that lay ahead must have become only too clear. As matters stood, the court was unlikely to find "good and sufficient proofs." What would the accusers in Stamford and Compo have to say about that?

· Six ·

"PERSISTING IN A
NON-AGREEMENT"

ON THE MORNING OF THURSDAY, 14 SEPTEMBER 1692, William Jones joined the other magistrates appointed to the special court at the meetinghouse in Fairfield to begin the long-awaited trial of Elizabeth Clawson and Mercy Disborough. Witnesses against the accused had traveled from Stamford and Compo to appear before the court—at stake was the well-being, perhaps even survival, of those who believed they had been bewitched. But friends as well as enemies of the witch suspects crowded into the meetinghouse—the lives of the accused also hung in the balance.

The meetinghouse in Fairfield was bigger than its counterpart in Stamford, but similar in design. A square building with no architectural frills, simple and functional in design, the setting in which the trials took place would have seemed quite familiar to those who had come from Stamford. But the witnesses were no longer speaking to local judges within their own community. Instead they must address a panel of great men from Hartford who sat in state on a raised platform. Witnesses from Compo, located just a few miles away, would mostly likely know the jurymen, who were chosen from among the male residents of Fairfield and its surrounding communities. But those who lived in Stamford, some fifteen miles away, were speaking for the most part in front of strangers.

The magistrates began by administering the oath of office to James Bennett and Eliphalet Hill, who would serve as prosecutors on behalf of the Crown. They then swore in members of the grand jury, whose task it was to determine whether the evidence against the accused was sufficient to justify going ahead with a trial. With regard to the allegations against Mary Staples, Mary Harvey, and Hannah Harvey, the jurymen took the view that there was sufficient evidence to proceed. But the magistrates disagreed and so dismissed the cases against all three. There was no disagreement about the bills of indictment against Elizabeth Clawson and Mercy Disborough, which the jurymen and magistrates approved without hesitation. William Jones and his colleagues now released the grand jury and swore in a separate trial jury whose task it was to determine whether Elizabeth Clawson and Mercy Disborough were guilty as charged.

The joint trial began with the reading aloud of the indictments. The prosecutors then presented their case. They and the magistrates questioned witnesses, who testified under oath, and also the accused. The defendants had no attorney and did not speak under oath, so their words did not necessarily carry the same credibility as those of witnesses. But they did have the right to cross-examine witnesses for the prosecution and they could call their own witnesses in an attempt to refute the charges against them. Once everyone had been heard, the jury withdrew to consider its verdict.

There is no surviving account of the mood in the meeting-house up to that point. The recent proceedings in Salem had often plunged into chaos as the afflicted girls claimed to be attacked by spectral tormentors: they fell to the floor, contorted in agony, and cried out in terror against their alleged assailants. Katherine Branch may well have been present at the trials in Fairfield, but it is also possible that the testimony she gave that spring was read to the jury instead of having her appear in person. Given how controversial a figure she was, the prosecutors might have decided to keep her in Stamford so as to focus attention on evidence given by other, more credible victims of the accused. If Kate was there, we have no way of knowing if she suffered from fits during the trials or, if so, how the magistrates, jurymen, or defendants reacted. Nor do we know how Elizabeth Clawson and Mercy Disborough behaved under interrogation. Some of the accused at Salem were defiant and outspoken; others were pious in their words and respectful in demeanor. Neither of the women on trial in Fairfield were submissive by temperament, but they may have decided that it would be politic on this occasion to restrain themselves.

One thing is certain, that as William Jones listened to the testimony given by witnesses in the meetinghouse, he cannot have heard anything that lessened his sense of foreboding as the jury retired to deliberate. The evidence was assuredly impressive in quantity, but its substance was problematic. It soon became clear that his concerns were fully justified. So far the trials had moved along quickly, as was the custom, but now they ground to a halt as the jury spent hour after hour debating the evidence without reaching any final resolution. The governor had instructed the jury to keep in mind the specific language used in the indictments. The defendants were each accused of "familiarity with Satan, the grand enemy of God and man." The jury must be confident that the accused had forsaken allegiance to God and formed an alliance with Satan. There lay the problem.

Not all of the jurymen were convinced that the two women were guilty of witchcraft. Even those who were convinced had to consider the discrepancy between the evidence they had heard and the terms of the indictment. The sticking point was the need for clear proof of the Devil's involvement since hardly any of the depositions mentioned dealings between Elizabeth Clawson or Mercy Disborough and "the grand enemy of God." The witnesses focused on who had a motive to inflict occult harm on the victims, not how the harm was inflicted or whether the Devil was involved. That made for a perplexing situation. Should the jury convict the women regardless of whether or not the evidence demonstrated "familiarity" with Satan? If Elizabeth Clawson and Mercy Disborough were clearly using dark cunning to bewitch those who crossed them, should the safety of their neighbors take precedence over legal niceties? Or should they adhere closely, as the magistrates evidently wanted, to the precise wording of the indictments?

As it became clear that the jury could not reach a unanimous decision on either case, the magistrates had to decide between three options. They could continue to wait, trusting that the jurymen would eventually reach a verdict of their own accord. But that seemed increasingly unlikely and in any case waiting indefinitely was impractical since the magistrates needed to leave Fairfield as soon as possible—these were men of substance with many other demands on their time. Given that there was no immediate prospect of resolution, a second option involved the magistrates stepping in to provide additional advice. But they had already given what they considered to be a clear and sufficient explanation of the law. Besides, interfering in a jury's deliberations was a serious and delicate matter.

A third option involved referring the cases back to Connecticut's representative assembly with a request for further guidance. The assembly had ultimate authority on judicial matters and was often referred to as the General Court. Adopting this expedient would in all likelihood mean bringing the special court back into session once the assembly gave its views on the case; and there was, furthermore, no guarantee that the assemblymen would say or do anything particularly helpful. But it would at least delay matters while the magistrates pondered their next move. The judges accordingly issued the following statement:

> The court having with long and much patience waited upon the jury to make verdicts upon the trial of the two prisoners Mercy Disborough and Elizabeth Clawson and after all endeavors the jury persisting in a non-agreement to a verdict wherein they may all agree, this court do see good reason to remand the prisoners to the common jail, there to be kept in safe custody till a return may be made to the General Court for further direction what shall be done in this matter and the gentlemen of the jury are also to be ready when further called by direction of the General Court to perfect their verdict. And if the attorneys for their Majesties find further testimony, they may have liberty to make further use of them when the court shall meet again.

The magistrates suspected that their expression of willingness to hear "further testimony" once the court reconvened was probably wishful thinking. As it turned out, a few additional testimonies did surface over the next few weeks, but they did not change the fundamental contours of the case. Magistrates, jurymen, and all those who awaited with concern the outcome of the trials must hope for enlightenment from the assembly.

Such enlightenment was not forthcoming. On 13 October, Governor Robert Treat gave members of the assembly in Hartford a detailed account of the court's proceedings and the jury's failure to agree on a verdict. The representatives were blunt in their response: they insisted that the special court must itself take responsibility for ensuring that the cases were resolved in a timely and judicious fashion. The special court was, after all, better acquainted than the assembly with the issues involved. The assemblymen accordingly passed a resolution asking the governor to "appoint a time for the said court to meet again as soon as may be, and that the jury be called together and that they make a verdict upon the case and the court to put a final issue thereto." The assembly offered no opinion or recommendation with regard to the cases under consideration.

This response came as no great surprise to the seven judges. Indeed they had already decided on their return from Fairfield to seek assistance from another quarter; namely, Connecticut's ministers. Most New England magistrates had no formal training in the law, much less the mysteries of the invisible world. Deputy-Governor Jones had prepared carefully for the joint trial, but even he may have doubted whether he grasped fully the finer points in the works he had read. Most ministers were, in sharp contrast, trained for their vocation either at Harvard College in Cambridge, Massachusetts, or at one of England's universities; there they acquired extensive learning and the specific knowledge with which to make sense of cases involving preternatural phenomena. The judges accordingly asked a group of ministers to meet in Hartford, read the depositions against the two women, and submit a written opinion. On 17 October, four days after the assembly resolved that the special court should resume its proceedings as soon as possible, Timothy Woodbridge, the pastor in Hartford for almost a decade, delivered to Governor Treat the ministers' report.

Mister Jones, who was doubtless eager to compare the ministers' recommendations with his own notes, must have read the document with a growing sense of assurance that he had understood the issues involved.

As to the evidences left to our consideration respecting the two women suspected of witchcraft at Fairfield, we offer:

1. That we cannot but give our concurrence with the generality of divines that the endeavor of conviction of witchcraft by swimming is unlawful and sinful and therefore it cannot afford any evidence.

This condemnation of ducking—or swimming, as the ministers put it—was entirely consistent with William Jones's own reading on the subject. He continued to read:

2. That the unusual excrescences found upon their bodies ought not to be allowed as evidence against them without the approbation of some able physicians.

Here was an interesting twist. The ministers accepted the Devil's mark as a basis for conviction, but also insisted that "able physicians"—by which the ministers meant male doctors—must confirm that the markings were "unusual" and in all likelihood diabolical. Elizabeth Clawson and Mercy Disborough had been searched for the Devil's mark on three separate occasions, but always by local women. Their examiners were experienced in midwifery and had intimate knowledge of the female body. But the ministers now argued that such expertise was insufficient. If the court abided by the ministers' advice, the only tangible evidence of Satan's involvement before the court would have to be deemed inadmissible.

In the third section of their response the ministers had much to say about Katherine Branch:

> 3. Respecting the evidence of the afflicted maid, we find some things testified carrying a suspicion of her counterfeiting, others that plainly intimate her trouble as coming from her mother, which improved by craft may produce most of those strange and unusual effects affirmed of her, and those things that by some may be thought to be diabolical or effects of witchcraft. We apprehend her applying of them to these persons merely from the appearance of their specters to her to be very uncertain and fallible from the easy deception of her senses and subtle devices of the Devil, wherefore we cannot think her a sufficient witness. Yet we think that her affliction, being something strange, well deserves a further inquiry.

The prospect of "further inquiry" must have made William Jones flinch, but in other respects this paragraph would have heartened the deputy-governor. Whereas Stamford's pastor, John Bishop, had quickly concluded that Kate's fits were the result of witchcraft, these ministers were much more skeptical. They were by no means alone in expressing doubts about the maidservant's claims: some of Kate's neighbors also suspected that her fits were staged; others recalled that her mother had suffered from similar symptoms and wondered if Kate's behavior was inherited. Perhaps, as the ministers suggested, her torments were a combination of involuntary fits and crafted performance. The deputy-governor must have noted that the statement included an unequivocal rejection of spectral evidence as a reliable basis for conviction. Katherine Branch's affliction was, they acknowledged, "something strange," but she was clearly not "a sufficient witness."

The ministers' final recommendation related to the bulk of the evidence against the accused:

> 4. As to the other strange accidents such as the dying of cattle, etc, we apprehend the applying of them to these women as matters of witchcraft to be upon very slender and uncertain grounds.

Here again the ministers confirmed William Jones's own understanding. No responsible court would send a suspect to the gallows based on cirumstantial evidence such as this.

William Jones must have been reassured by the consistency of his own notes with this report, compiled by learned men of God. The ministers did not reject the possibility that Elizabeth Clawson and Mercy Disborough were witches, but they did repudiate the evidence before the court as a sound basis for conviction. Their advice would provide an important reinforcement as Mister Jones and his fellow magistrates urged caution upon the jury.

On 28 October 1692, the court reconvened in Fairfield. The meetinghouse was again packed with local residents, relatives and friends of the defendants, and those who had testified against the accused. The atmosphere must have been electric with anticipation. After the proceedings were called to order, the governor once again instructed the jury to leave the room in order to reach a verdict, starting with Mercy Disborough. Were the jurymen told about the ministers' recommendations? Was the ministers' report read out loud in court? We do not know. But the governor doubtless reminded members of the jury that their decision must be based on the precise wording of the indictment against the defendant. When the jurymen returned (we do not know how long they took), the nervous whispers of the crowd must have faded into silence as the governor asked the jury to deliver its verdict. The jury spokesman announced that they found Mercy Disborough "guilty according to the indictment."

This was not what William Jones and his colleagues had expected. Other than the supernatural markings, there was no clear indication that Mercy Disborough had formed an alliance with the Devil; and no male physician had authenticated the markings as diabolical. After conferring briefly with his fellow magistrates, the governor reminded the jurymen that they could convict with a clear conscience only if they found indisputable evidence of "familiarity with Satan." He sent them back to reconsider their verdict.

When the jurymen returned, they declared that they saw "no reason to alter their verdict" and found Mercy Disborough guilty as before. The judges again took counsel. The consistent opinion of women who examined Goody Disborough's body that she had supernatural markings, in combination with other evidence against her, must have swayed the jury. Should they accept that physical evidence as grounds for conviction, even though no male physician had confirmed what the women said? The ministers had urged otherwise, but surely in matters such as these experienced goodwives could be trusted. The magistrates decided, albeit reluctantly, to approve the verdict and Governor Treat proceeded to deliver the prescribed sentence:

> Mercy Disborough, you have been found guilty of the felonies and witchcrafts whereof you stand indicted. The court now passes sentence of death upon you as the law directs. You shall be carried from this place to the gaol from whence you came, and from thence to the place of execution, and there hang till you be dead. May the Lord have mercy on your soul.

As he listened to the sentence, the deputy-governor doubtless cast his eyes over the courtroom to see the reaction of those in attendance. If Daniel Wescot was seated among the spectators, what did his facial expression reveal? Grim satisfaction? It was the fate of his neighbor Goody Clawson that Wescot was most eager to hear, but the judgment against Mercy Disborough would have given him encouragement.

The jurymen then left the room to consider the case of Goody Clawson. They returned to pronounce her "not guilty according to the indictment." The judges must have been much relieved. The failure of repeated searches to find a Devil's mark on Goody Clawson's body would have made it impossible to support a conviction. Overturning a jury's verdict was always a serious busi-

WITCHES BEING HANGED   *Contrary to popular mythology, witches in England and New England were hanged, not burned, either from scaffolds as shown here or from trees. It is no coincidence that all seven of the condemned witches shown here were women. Though a sizeable minority of those accused on both sides of the Atlantic were men, women were much more vulnerable to witch accusations (four-fifths of those accused in seventeenth-century New England were female).*   (SOURCE: FROM RALPH GARDINER, *ENGLAND'S GRIEVANCE DISCOVERED* [1655].)

ness and doing so would have angered those convinced of Elizabeth Clawson's guilt even more than a straightforward acquittal. The magistrates approved the verdict and ordered Goody Clawson's release from jail.

When witch trials ended in acquittal, New England magistrates sometimes urged accusers to accept the verdict with good grace and to leave the defendant unmolested on condition that she did likewise. At the end of a previous trial in Connecticut, the court had instructed neighbors to "carry neighborly and peaceably, without unjust offence" to the accused and her family. In September 1692, on dismissing the allegations against Goody Staples and the Harveys, Governor Treat had "commanded" all concerned "to forbear speaking evil of the foresaid persons for the future upon pain of displeasure." There is no record of whether the magistrates issued a similar "command" now that Elizabeth Clawson was to be set free. But we can imagine Mister Jones rising from his chair, gathering his papers as he prepared to leave the meetinghouse, and turning to see Daniel Wescot still seated on his bench, rigid and stony-faced: this cannot have been the verdict that he wanted or expected. And the expressions of other Stamford residents may also have suggested that any call for "neighborly and peaceable" behavior toward the Clawsons, however well intentioned, might be unrealistic.

However unenthusiastic they may have been about the verdict against Goody Disborough, Mister Jones and his fellow magistrates must at least have been pleased to leave Fairfield with two unequivocal judgments on record. But any notion they may have had that the witch trials were now over was premature. Within days, a group of Mercy Disborough's supporters submitted a petition pointing out that one of the original jurors from the September trial had failed to attend the second session in October because he was away on business. Someone else had been appointed to serve in his place. The petitioners argued that this substitution was illegal and that therefore the conviction should be overturned. The General Court appointed a committee of three magistrates (Samuel Wyllys, William Pitkin, and Nathaniel Stanley) to investigate the claim, empowering them to "take such action as they saw fit." Meanwhile, Mercy Disborough was granted a stay of execution.

Six long months passed before the three magistrates submitted their report. Then, as now, the wheels of justice could turn all too slowly for those under confinement. Goody Disborough had now been imprisoned for almost a year. When the report finally arrived in May 1693, William Jones must have worried as he made his way to the governor's house: if the committee had sided with the petitioners, it would be highly embarrassing for him and the other judges. Sure enough, the report declared that the jury change was illegal:

> It is so inviolable a practice in law that the individual jurors charged with the deliverance of a prisoner in a capital case and on whom the prisoner puts him or herself to be tried must try the case, and they only, that all the precedents in Old England and New confirm it. And not only precedent but the nature of the commission enforces it, for to these jurors the law gave this power and vested it in them. They had it by right of law. It is incompatible and impossible that it should be vested in these and in others too, for then two juries may have the same power in the same case. One man altered, the jury is altered.

The committee insisted that the court's proceedings must be free from any irregularity, even if the defendant was clearly guilty, "lest they bring themselves and the whole county into inextricable troubles." "Due form of law," they wrote, "is that alone wherein the validity of verdicts and judgments in such cases stands. And if a real and apparent murderer be condemned and executed out of due form of law, it is indictable against them that do it, for in such a case the law is superceded by arbitrary doings." All those involved in adjudicating this case should "take heed that what they do now will be rolled to their door." The report concluded with a dramatic declaration: "Blood is a great thing and we cannot but open our mouths for the dumb in the cause of one appointed to die by such a verdict." The deputy-governor may well have blanched on reading these words: "what they do now will be rolled to their door." In convicting a murderer without due process, the authors were hinting, those responsible were themselves guilty of murder.

But the three magistrates voiced an additional concern. None of the evidence presented against Mercy Disborough could, in their view, satisfy the criteria laid down by experts such as "Mr. Perkins, Mr. Bernard, and Mr. Mather" so as to be "sufficiently convictive of witchcraft." The magistrates specified the same grounds for conviction that William Jones had entered into his notes prior to the trial: either confession or "two good witnesses proving some act or acts done by the person which could not be but by help of the Devil." "This there was none of," they declared succinctly.

"As for the common things of spectral evidence, ill events after quarrels or threats, teats, water trials, and the like," the report continued, these were "all discarded and some of them abominated by the most judicious as to be convictive of witchcraft." The committee also pointed to the grim lesson provided by recent events in Salem: "the miserable toil" in which the Massachusetts court found itself for convicting defendants on the basis of dubious evidence should be "warning enough" to the magistrates in Connecticut dealing with Goody Disborough's case. "Those who will make witchcraft of such things will make hanging work apace," they declared, "and we are informed of no other but such kinds of evidence brought against this woman."

Accordingly, the three magistrates reprieved Mercy Disborough from being put to death until the assembly could reconsider her case in the light of their findings. It would have to decide, they wrote, "how far these proceedings do put a difficulty on any further trial of this woman."

And, indeed, in due time, the assembly would follow the report's recommendation by acquitting Mercy Disborough and ordering her release. But what if Mercy Disborough *was* a witch? How could the court protect those who had accused her from the threat of retribution? And what if she was truly innocent? Who could protect her from the anger and resentment of neighbors who were so anxious to have her removed?

Ever since her arrest in June 1692, Mercy Disborough had faced the threat of execution; that threat was finally removed, and she was free to go. There is, unfortunately, no record of what happened on the day that Mercy Disborough was released from her year of imprisonment. Perhaps a crowd gathered to watch her emerge from the jail—some of the onlookers sympathetic, others sullen or even loudly hostile. Perhaps Thomas Disborough anticipated such a response and came for his wife at first light when the street would be empty, the first moments of their reunion undisturbed by curious bystanders. Perhaps he embraced his wife and helped her to their cart, where they sat side by side, husband and wife, for the first time since her arrest. Perhaps she turned to him and smiled as she realized that at long last she was going home.

But such intimate knowledge is far beyond our scope. Goodman Disborough may have greeted his wife coldly, resentful of all she had cost him in respect and money. (As was the custom, he had to pay all fees and prison charges for the period of her confinement, even though she had been acquitted.) They may have ridden homeward in stony silence. And any pleasure Goody Disborough took in observing the open fields and ripening crops along the road may have been overshadowed by a sense of foreboding as to what awaited her in Compo.

Mercy Disborough was alive and free, but were her troubles over? A decade earlier a woman in Massachusetts had been acquitted of witchcraft. But a year or so later neighbors suspected her of striking again when an elderly man in the town fell ill. One night a group of young men visited the woman: they dragged her outside, hanged her from a tree until she seemed to be gasping her last breath, then cut her down, rolled her in the snow, and buried her in it, leaving her for dead. Amazingly, she survived, though barely. The law was only one way of dealing with a witch . . .

AFTERWORD

I<small>F</small> M<small>ERCY</small> D<small>ISBOROUGH DID WORRY THAT HER RELEASE FROM</small> prison might not end her ordeal, later events proved her fears to be well founded. On 3 June 1696, the Reverend Gershom Bulkeley of Wethersfield, Connecticut, wrote a letter to his nephew, Joseph Bulkeley, a Fairfield resident and relative of Mercy's. The minister was writing to clear Goody Disborough of a slander recently cast on her by one James Redfin. Before her marriage to Thomas Disborough, Mercy (then Holbridge) had lived for a while with the Reverend Bulkeley in New London. According to James Redfin, Mercy was pregnant at the time and several months later, after moving to Wethersfield with the minister, gave birth to an illegitimate child. The father of the child, Redfin claimed, was "a great man" and so "it was smothered up."[1]

The Reverend Gershom Bulkeley, who realized that "the scandal" arising from James Redfin's allegations reflected on him as well as Mercy, insisted that this was "a most malicious lie from the beginning to the end of it." She had indeed lived with him in New London, but her behavior had been "blameless and inoffensive." When he moved to Wethersfield, Mercy did not go with him. This was actually a case of mistaken identity, the pastor explained: another young woman, named Elizabeth Walker, who also lived in the house did ("to my grief") turn out to be pregnant. The minister had purchased Elizabeth as an indentured servant in Boston. She gave birth in Wethersfield, but the baby died soon afterward. There were suspicions about the cause of death, but a formal investigation cleared her. The alleged father, Bulkeley added, was at the time "no great man," appeared in court to answer Elizabeth's charge of paternity, and denied having fathered the child.

Gershom Bulkeley was convinced that Mercy Disborough's enemies, driven by "bloody malice" and "having by a good Providence missed their mark of taking away her life by one project [accusing her of witchcraft in 1692], would now do it, if possible, by another [having her tried for infanticide, also a capital offense]." But Thomas and Mercy Disborough had seized the initiative and sued James Redfin for slander. The Reverend Bulkeley was writing to refute Redfin's claims and to support the case against him. He told his nephew that he could show the letter to whomever he pleased, "if it may be any ways beneficial." The pastor warned that "wise men, who would not imbrue their hands in blood," should "take heed how they give ear to such malicious liars, lest they be partakers of their sin."

The formal record of this slander case does not survive, but evidently Goody Disborough was not left in peace following her acquittal of witchcraft in 1693. Just over a decade after she and her husband accused James Redfin of slander, Thomas Disborough died. His precise date of death is not known, but the local court recorded the inventory of his estate in March 1709, at which time the magistrates granted Mercy, as was the custom, a portion of the property as his widow; the couple's only son received the balance. How long Mercy lived after that we do not know: there is no surviving record of her death.[2]

During the months and years that followed Elizabeth Clawson's acquittal, she neither did nor said anything that survived in the historical record, though we do know that she spent the rest of her life in Stamford with her family. Her husband Stephen died around 1700. A record of Elizabeth Clawson's death does survive: she passed away on 10 May 1714, at the age of eighty-three.[3]

What was Goody Clawson's life like in the aftermath of her ordeal? Did she forgive the women and men whose hostile testimony brought her so close to death? Or did she bear a grudge and, if so, how much of an effort did she make to conceal her resentment? Were those neighbors who still believed her guilty willing to behave "neighborly and peaceably" toward her? Would they avoid her for fear of arousing a witch's anger, or look for opportunities to gather further evidence against her? Was there tension between those who had supported Goody Clawson during the trial and those who believed in her guilt? And, if so, how long did it linger?

Unfortunately, no information survives that would enable us to answer such questions. Most accused witches made a brief and dramatic appearance in the records at the time of their trial and then returned to obscurity once the ordeal was over. The transcripts from witch trials often seem like narrow-beamed spotlights that play upon an otherwise darkened landscape. What happened after the trial ended is in most cases a mystery, unless the defendant was condemned to death (and even then we do not always know for certain that the sentence was carried out) or unless the accused was acquitted and then put on trial again at some later date. The silence of the records regarding Elizabeth Clawson's life after her release is, then, not unusual. It does tell us that whatever tensions remained in Stamford, they did not reach a level of intensity requiring formal intervention by the courts. That does not mean, of course, that Elizabeth Clawson and her family never encountered hostility from members of their community—but whatever tensions there were went unrecorded.

Reconstructing what happened before or even during a trial for witchcraft can prove equally challenging. In most cases we cannot be sure that we have all the official papers and in some instances only a few depositions or none at all have survived. Even relatively complete court transcripts rarely provide all the information that we would like to have about the context from which an accusation emerged. Other sources sometimes shed light on the history of growing suspicion that culminated—often after many years—in a formal charge of witchcraft. Accusers and the accused may have been involved in earlier disputes described in court records, the minutes from town meetings, or church records. But for every useful piece of information that historians unearth, there remain many questions that cannot be answered. This is particularly true of suspects and accusers who were women: far fewer women than men could write and thus leave behind diaries or letters; women were, moreover, much less likely to engage in commercial transactions or public activities that were likely to be recorded. But most nonelite men present similar challenges: the day-to-day details of their lives also went largely undocumented and so we have to rely on the often incomplete trial records.

Some documents are more tantalizing than revealing. Consider the petition defending Elizabeth Clawson, signed by seventy-six residents of Stamford. Bearing in mind that the total population of the town was only around five hundred, that most of the town residents lived in close proximity to one another, and that by the end of the seventeenth century many families had intermarried, we might well wonder how signing the petition affected the lives of Goody Clawson's supporters. But we do not have that kind of information. We do not even have a map showing where each family lived in the late seventeenth century. One of the signers, Stephen Bishop, was the Reverend John Bishop's son. How did Stamford's pastor react to his son signing the petition? It is striking that John Bishop did not give testimony before the court (unless it has been lost). The minister had, after all, visited the Wescots' home to offer counsel and support, yet he does not seem to have shared with the court his impression of what had happened to Kate. Was he anxious to avoid becoming embroiled in the witch hunt because it had already caused so much division within the town? Did he not believe Kate's specific accusations? Did Stephen have his father's blessing in supporting Elizabeth Clawson? Or was the minister convinced of Goody Clawson's guilt and angered by his son's position? Was he perhaps also worried by Stephen's becoming so openly involved in the controversy over Kate's claims? John Bishop's silence would be intriguing enough even if the petition did not exist, but the presence of his son's signature on the petition raises many more questions that cannot be answered.

In sharp contrast, the survival of a memorandum in the hand of Deputy-Governor Jones, summarizing his notes taken from books that gave advice on the prosecution of witches, constitutes an extraordinary gift. That document enabled me to reconstruct how one magistrate presiding over the trials would have reacted to the evidence presented in court and it provided a framing device for Chapter 5. The transcripts of depositions given by neighbors of the accused are also invaluable, providing detailed and richly colored vignettes of the social and cultural world that early New Englanders inhabited. Many of the depositions were given by townsfolk and villagers who could not write themselves but who gave oral testimony that was then recorded for the court. We should bear in mind that whoever recorded that testimony may have added or deleted words either by accident or based on their own whims; but most scholars agree that the transcripts from trials in early New England provide a fairly accurate record of what people actually said. These documents present us with a rare opportunity to "listen" as ordinary folk described the pattern of their lives, their interactions and arguments with each other, their fears, and their belief in the supernatural. Their words and the stories they told are the building blocks for this book.

TELLING THE STORY

In relating the chain of events that led to the Connecticut witch trials of 1692, my primary goal has been to reconstruct the ways in which New Englanders responded to mysterious "afflictions" and why many of them came to believe that such afflictions were caused by witchcraft. Most of us today would react quite differently and it is perhaps tempting to dismiss the reactions and beliefs described in this book as superstitious or ignorant. Yet New Englanders interpreted ailments or mishaps as malicious acts of witchcraft not because they were less enlightened or innately intelligent than us but because their culture taught them to do so. Explaining illness or misfortune in terms of witchcraft made good sense to early New Englanders, given the ways in which they viewed and experienced the world around them.

If we are to understand why an accusation of witchcraft would have seemed neither peculiar nor unreasonable to people living in a premodern society, we have to set aside our own ways of looking at the world and imagine it through their eyes. The court transcripts make that possible: in recording what witnesses said about the accused, they enable us to become time travelers, embarking on a journey into the lives and minds of seventeenth-century New Englanders.

Given that this book is largely about how people reacted to what they saw and heard, I have sought to reconstruct their observations, remarks, and conversations as faithfully as possible from the depositions. Take, for example, the midwife Sarah Bates's response to Katherine Branch's fits. The original transcript of her testimony reads as follows:

The Testimony of Mrs Sarah Bates she saith yt when first ye garl was taken with strang fitts she was sent for to Danll Wescots house & she found ye garl lieing upon ye Bed she then did aprehend yt the garls illnes might be from som naturall cause: she therfore advised them to burn feathers under her nose & other menes yt had dun good in fainting fits and then she seemed to be better with it:

and so she left her that night in hopes to here she wold be better ye next morning: but in ye morning Danll Wescot came for her againe and when she came she found ye garl in bed seemingly sence-les & spechless: her eyes half shut but her pulse semed to beat af-ter ye ordinary maner her mistres desired she might be let blud on ye foot in hopes it might do her good then I said I thought it could not be dun in ye capassity she was in but she desired a trial to be made and when every thing was redy & we were a going to let her blud ye garle cried: the reson was asked her why she cried: her An-swer was she would not be bludded: we asked her why: she said again because it would hurt her it was said ye hurt would be but small like ye prick of a pin then she put her foot over ye bed and was redy to help about it: this cariag of her seemed to me strang who before seemed to ly like a dead creature: after she was blud-ded and had laid a short time she clapt her hand upon ye coverlid and cried out and on of ye garls yt stood by said mother she cried out: and her mistres was so afected with it yt she cried and said she is bewitched: upon this ye garl turned her head from ye folk as if she wold hide it in ye pillow & laughed.

On first reading the court transcripts, I was immediately drawn to this dense paragraph in which the court clerk recorded Goody Bates's testimony. Here, it seemed to me, were the words of an observant and astute woman who had much of interest to say not only about Kate herself but also the family with whom she lived. Drawing out the implications of what she said about her two visits to the Wescot household and her evolving prognosis of Kate's condition involved several stages of adaptation. I be-gan by modernizing the text, which, like most court depositions from this period, is somewhat idiosyncratic in grammar and spelling. Filling out contractions, adopting modern spellings, and inserting additional punctuation produced the following version:

The Testimony of Mrs. Sarah Bates

She saith that when first the girl was taken with strange fits she was sent for to Daniel Wescot's house and she found the girl lying upon the bed. She then did apprehend that the girl's illness might be from some natural cause: she therefore advised them to burn feathers under her nose and other means that had done good in fainting fits and then she seemed to be better with it. And so she left her that night in hopes to hear she would be better the next morning. But in the morning Daniel Wescot came for her again, and when she came she found the girl in bed seemingly senseless and speechless, her eyes half shut but her pulse seemed to beat after the ordinary manner. Her mistress desired she might be let blood on the foot in hopes it might do her good. Then I said I thought it could not be done in the capacity she was in, but she desired a trial to be made and when everything was ready and we were a going to let her blood the girl cried. The reason was asked her why she cried: her answer was she would not be blooded. We asked her why: she said again because it would hurt her. It was said the hurt would be but small, like the prick of a pin. Then she put her foot over the bed and was ready to help about it. This carriage of hers seemed to me strange who before seemed to lie like a dead creature. After she was blooded and had laid a short time, she clapped her hand upon the coverlid and cried out. And one of the girls that stood by said, "Mother, she cried out!" And her mistress was so affected with it that she cried and said, "She is bewitched." Upon this the girl turned her head from the folk as if she would hide it in the pillow and laughed.

I then used the information contained within that adapted text to reconstruct in a section of Chapter 1 what happened during those two visits from Sarah Bates's point of view. I added some background information on the range of a midwife's knowledge, where that knowledge came from, and the assumptions that underlay treatments such as bleeding. But my description of her visits makes no attempt to provide an "objective" account of what was "really" happening in the Wescot household. Indeed it is not so much an account of "what happened" as a narration of what Goody Bates saw and how she reacted. I fleshed out her testimony so as to clarify the direction of her thoughts as I understood them, but the objective throughout was to build on her own words. Only in the final paragraph of that section did I depart from what Sarah Bates actually said to speculate about her thoughts as she noticed Kate laughing into her pillow:

> Goody Bates did not know what to think. Was Kate convinced that her sickness was natural and so surreptitiously laughing at her mistress for thinking that she was bewitched? Or was she faking her symptoms and enjoying her success in duping the Wescots? Or was the laugh itself a symptom of her fits? Determining the true cause of Kate's behavior was not going to be easy.

Yet even here the questions that I had the midwife ask herself were based closely on what other townsfolk were saying to each other during those fateful weeks.

Passages describing the circulation of gossip about Kate's afflictions and the misfortunes that followed quarrels involving Elizabeth Clawson or Mercy Disborough are also based closely on the depositions. Witnesses often acknowledged quite openly that the information they were reporting had passed through a chain of conversations in the neighborhood. Henry Grey, for example, told the court "that he hath been informed by some of his neighbors that Mercy Disborough hath at times discoursed with the wife of Thomas Benit, Sr., and [her] daughter, that the said Mercy Disborough said she could not abide the said Henry Grey ever since he bought a parcel of apples of her mother Mrs. Jones and reported that they wanted of measure, which was about eighteen years since." I have in a few passages taken some dramatic license in evoking for readers the situations in which such gossip would have been shared by neighbors. I do not know, for example, if John Finch, Mary Newman, and the Penoirs did have the conversation with which I begin Chapter 4, but what I have them say in that passage is taken directly from their court testimony and it is hardly a stretch to envisage Stamford residents sharing such stories as they discussed the allegations brought against Goody Clawson by the Wescots and their servant.

Each of the chapters in this book examines a particular phase of the witch hunt from the perspective of those who had a stake in what was happening. For most of those involved the transcripts provide at least some clues as to how they reacted as the crisis unfolded before them. The one significant exception is Katherine Branch. Kate became the object of horrified curiosity as neighbors visited the Wescot household to observe her fits and to help look after her. Her master and other Stamford residents later described the progression of her torments to court officials and repeated her allegations as to who was afflicting her. Kate herself was questioned by the magistrates, but only after several weeks of debate about the nature and cause of her condition, both inside the Wescot household and throughout Stamford, which may well have shaped what she said to court officials. All that we know about Kate's initial response to her fits came from those watching over her. We do know about the varied responses of neighbors to what was happening in the Wescot household; we know that Abigail Wescot believed her household to be bewitched and yet considered her servant to be a liar who could twist Daniel Wescot around her little finger; we know that Daniel Wescot boasted of the control that he had over his servant and that some people wondered what that meant. But Kate's actual condition and her motives for making the accusations remain a mystery.

One of my first decisions when embarking upon this project was to retain that sense of mystery. It is, of course, tempting to speculate. Did Kate really have epileptic fits? Today this would be diagnosed as a medical condition and treated accordingly. Even in the seventeenth century, doctors argued that fits could have physical causes, yet many assumed that symptoms such as Kate exhibited could also be brought about by supernatural means. There was much debate and confusion over which kinds of fits resulted from a physical disease and which from occult attack. The ministers' written opinion noted that Kate's mother had suffered from fits similar to those that afflicted Kate in 1692, a tantalizing snippet of information. What did Kate, who was no doctor, make of her condition? And how was she affected by the frightened reactions of those watching over her? We will, most likely, never know.

It is possible that Kate's torments were a sham, in which case she seems to have enjoyed deceiving her master and mistress: recall Sarah Bates's description of Kate turning away from the family and laughing into her pillow. The laughter may have been hysterical. But even if so, even if Kate's fits were largely involuntary, and even if she believed quite sincerely that she was bewitched, there may also have been a element of feigning. After all, the fits transformed an insignificant servant into a local phenomenon: Kate became the center of attention not only within the Wescot household but throughout Stamford and beyond. As she began to accuse specific women of bewitching her, Kate may well have been prompted by her master and mistress to name particular individuals, but it was Kate who made the accusations. In doing so, she wielded tremendous power. It might be tempting to envisage Kate as an embittered and rebellious teenager, resentful of her position in the Wescot household and now reveling in her sudden acquisition of power; or alternatively as a young woman eager to please her perhaps beguiling and beguiled master.

In each of these possible scenarios the boundary between performance and sincere belief was most likely blurred. In a world where everyone believed in the supernatural, what began as pretense may have ended up scaring the deceiver—feigning may have slid imperceptibly into terrified belief. Nor did Kate become empowered in any straightforward or complete sense. To be sure, she consigned her alleged tormenters to jail and potentially the gallows. Yet the women whom she accused were not, after all, her own enemies but those of her master and mistress; Kate was, in a sense, exacting revenge on the Wescots' behalf even as she turned their world upside down and became the center of their lives.

But all this is mere speculation. To settle on a particular interpretation of Kate's behavior strikes me as problematic, not only because of the lack of evidence but also because people at the time were clearly uncertain and divided as to whether Kate was bewitched and if her allegations against specific women could be trusted. That uncertainty was a key component of the situation and has to be retained if we are going to understand just how perplexing Kate's ordeal was for those around her. There swirled around Kate a maelstrom of sensational images and reports, but at the center of it all was an enigma.

We know almost nothing about Kate's prior history. One deposition claimed that she was French. If so, it is puzzling that no one else mentioned her nationality, especially given English hostility toward the French at the time. It was certainly not unknown for New Englanders to blacken the names of those they disliked or feared by invoking their national or regional origin, ethnicity, race, or religious affiliation. In 1688, when Mary Glover was tried and executed as a witch in Boston, her identity as a Gaelic-speaking Irish Catholic was clearly an issue. Puritans believed Catholics to be servants of the Antichrist and France was officially a Catholic country. But even if Kate's family was French, it was not necessarily Catholic: French migrants to British colonies in North America were often Huguenot Protestants.[4]

Nor do we know anything about what happened to Kate after the witch trials. Her master served again as Stamford's representative to the colonial assembly in May and October 1694, but the family later moved away with a group of migrants from Fairfield County to resettle in Cohancey, New Jersey, where Daniel Wescot died in 1704.[5] It is possible that the Wescots found their position in Stamford problematic in the aftermath of their neighbor's trial. Many townsfolk believed Elizabeth Clawson to be guilty as charged, but the petition on her behalf made it abundantly clear that many others did not. Daniel Wescot's reelection as representative in 1694 indicates that he did not become a pariah in the town, but he and his family must have figured prominently in tensions and recriminations that followed Goody Clawson's acquittal. Whether Kate accompanied the Wescots to New Jersey is unclear; she simply fades into oblivion.

During 1692, Katherine Branch became a slate on which the people of Stamford could etch their own fears, doubts, and convictions. She figured in the witch hunt not as a person in her own right but as an object of horror and pity, as a representation of the afflictions undergone by other townsfolk, and as an inspiration for those who wanted to strike back at those responsible for their torments by accusing them. Though we cannot know for certain what Kate was experiencing, we can at least watch the residents of Stamford as they watched her and pondered the meaning of her condition. That in turn helps us to understand how New England towns dealt with the threat that witchcraft seemed to pose.

The challenge of relating for a modern audience the ways in which Kate's neighbors reacted to her fits takes us to the very heart of this book and my reasons for writing it. In particular I wanted to capture the blend of supernatural belief and deliberate caution that underlay responses to Kate's condition. New Englanders believed wholeheartedly in an invisible world and the reality of witchcraft. Yet they did not immediately or without question accept claims that a particular person was bewitched or that a specific individual was responsible. Proponents of new scientific theories and methods in the late seventeenth and eighteenth centuries (the so-called scientific revolution) often contrasted their own experimental and reasoned approach with theological models for understanding the world, which they derided as based on blind faith and superstition. We should, however, beware of accepting that contrast at face value: it was, after all, self-serving. Interpretation based on careful observation and rationality was not quite so innovative as propagandists for these new scientific paradigms claimed. Theological discussions of witchcraft and other supernatural phenomena throughout the medieval and early modern periods were usually framed as logical arguments and supported by a large body of evidence, gathered from witnesses and the interrogation of witch suspects: they were self-consciously rational and empirical.

Popular beliefs and accusations were also based on a good deal more than fantasy or the unquestioning acceptance of far-fetched tales. People questioned closely neighbors who claimed to be bewitched; their assumptions and conclusions were based on what they perceived as actual experience. At every stage of the Stamford witch hunt, neighbors and officials were eager to test Kate's claims through careful observation and experimentation. I have sought to show on the one hand how cautious most of those involved were as they sought to confirm or refute suspicions of witchcraft through the scrupulous collection of evidence, while retaining on the other hand a sense of their belief in the reality of malign occult forces and their fear at the prospect of having to confront them. The assumptions from which these New Englanders proceeded and the specific techniques that they used may strike us as bizarre, yet they were clearly committed to a process of empirical verification that we might perhaps characterize as scientific supernaturalism.

At stake were human lives—those of the accused and their accusers—which brings me to my other motive for writing this book. I wanted to tell a story that I find gripping and moving, a story that surely deserves to be told; and I wanted to bring to life for readers the world in which it took place. Most academic studies of New England witchcraft assume the "objective" voice of the historian who looks back on events and analyzes them. This book seeks to recreate the world in which the people of Stamford and Compo lived by giving them voice, avoiding the deliberate self-distancing inherent in most scholarly analysis. I wanted to get as close as possible to their lives, their points of view, and their fears. I was aided in that task by the trial depositions, which are *narrative-driven* and *perspective-driven* in their format. What I mean by that is that witnesses told stories about personal experiences that seemed significant to them, often in vivid detail, and along the way made clear their interpretation of the incidents in question. What emerges is a constellation of narratives, each with its own context, perspective, and motivation.

The way in which we choose to tell a story is, of course, influenced by our own point of view—and that applies to historians as well as those who speak to us through surviving documents. My retelling of this particular story has been shaped by my own interpretive stance as a scholar of New England witchcraft and also by my reading of books and articles written by other historians. Recent scholars have used the transcripts from witch trials as a window into the lives and attitudes of ordinary colonists whose voices are otherwise lost to us. These scholars have reconstructed the supernatural beliefs that influenced townsfolk as they began to suspect that one of their neighbors was a witch and the local tensions that found expression in the form of witch accusations. Their findings and interpretations have informed my choices as a storyteller. The scholarship that undergirds this narrative remains for the most part implicit throughout the main body of the book: the story itself and its characters occupy center stage. But now the time has come to lay out much more explicitly the approaches and interpretations that have guided my account of how the residents of Stamford and Compo reacted to a young woman who claimed she was bewitched.

A WORLD OF WONDERS

As historian Keith Thomas pointed out in his classic study of English witch beliefs, *Religion and the Decline of Magic*, the anxieties that led to witch accusations "reflected the hazards of an intensely insecure environment."[6] We are raised to believe that modern technologies enable us to control our environment and solve our medical problems. Such confidence is not without foundation: when it gets dark, we turn on electric lights and so banish the darkness; when we fall ill, medicinal and surgical therapies can often either cure us or at least control our symptoms. Seventeenth-century men and women did not enjoy that same degree of control or confidence. Medical experts were, as Thomas points out, "quite unable to diagnose or treat most contemporary illnesses."[7] In general, much that we claim to understand was for the members of premodern society incomprehensible and uncontrollable—save in supernatural terms.

Seventeenth-century New Englanders believed that their world was filled with supernatural forces that could bring about physical effects. When Abraham Finch thought he saw a ball of fire pass through Katherine Branch's room and believed Kate's explanation that a woman with "fiery eyes" had come into the room, when Edward Jesop could not push a canoe into the creek and suspected that Mercy Disborough had bewitched it, and when Goodwife Newman concluded that the sudden death of three sheep was due to witchcraft, their reactions would not have struck contemporaries as peculiar. For all the Puritans' determination to break with the "superstitions" of the past, especially those associated with the Catholic Church, they were just as convinced as other English folk on both sides of the Atlantic that the universe was an enchanted place. New England colonists, writes historian David D. Hall, "remained Elizabethans" and inhabited "a world of wonders."[8] The supernatural realm, they believed, could intrude upon their lives at any time. Any extraordinary event that seemed to interrupt the natural order—comets and eclipses, dramatic fires and epidemics, deformed births and inexplicable crop failures, dreams and visions—carried supernatural significance. Some were sent by God, others by Satan.

According to the world view embraced by most New Englanders, God and the Devil were constantly at work in their day-to-day lives, testing and tempting, rewarding and punishing as each son and daughter of Adam and Eve deserved. God had ultimate authority over all that occurred in the universe, so that when the Devil intervened in people's lives, he was able to do so because God allowed it to happen. Ministers argued that any misfortune or mishap carried a divine message: usually God was prompting sinners to self-examination, repentance, and a renewed commitment to obey God's commandments. On some occasions God inflicted the warning himself; on others he allowed the Devil or even a human witch to act on his behalf. In either case, ministers insisted that the appropriate response was to repent and reform. When Puritan tailor John Dane was stung by an insect and his arm became badly swollen, he accordingly "prayed earnestly to God that He would pardon my sin and heal my arm." Dane also sought a medical prognosis from a devout physician, who declared his condition to be "the take." When the young man asked him what that meant, he replied, "it was taken by the providence of God." According to the doctor, John Dane was being punished for his sins and must mend his ways in order for the affliction to be removed.[9]

Yet godly New Englanders looked outward as well as inward for the source of their afflictions. When girls and young women in Salem Village began to suffer strange fits, the minister Samuel Parris at first prescribed prayer and fasting; he also consulted a physician. But once both men became convinced that witchcraft was causing the torments, Samuel Parris encouraged the afflicted to name their tormentors so that they could be brought to justice. There was nothing unorthodox about such a strategy: as the Bible declared, "Thou shalt not suffer a witch to live." Scripture taught that witches were real and that they should be hunted down for punishment. Yet biblical mandate and resentment of the damage inflicted by witches were not the only reasons why colonists reacted to afflictions by lashing out against those apparently responsible for their adversities.

Alongside Protestant Christianity there survived and flourished in New England less formal and yet influential folk beliefs that the settlers brought from England, including those that underlay the use of magic. Folk magic was based on the assumption that men and women could wield supernatural power for their own benefit. Many settlers believed that through the use of simple techniques, passed down from one generation to the next, they could harness occult forces so as to achieve greater knowledge and control over their lives. Experts in these techniques—often called "cunning folk"—told fortunes, claimed to heal the sick, and offered protection against witchcraft. But cunning folk could also use their skills for malevolent ends: to harm or destroy those who crossed them. Neighbors who possessed occult powers were thus valuable allies, but also potentially deadly enemies.

Most divining, healing, and defensive techniques were quite straightforward and so it was not unusual for colonists to experiment on their own. But New Englanders did often turn to experts in times of need, hoping that cunning folk could help them to see into the future, heal their ailments, or defend them against supernatural attack and strike back at their enemies. Mary Sibley, aunt of one of the afflicted children in Salem Village, asked the minister's Caribbean slave, Tituba, to bake a urine-cake that would identify the witch responsible for afflicting her niece; Tituba had a reputation for magical cunning and claimed that "her mistress in her own country . . . had taught her some means to be used for the discovery of a witch."[10]

Transcripts from the Connecticut trials of 1692 make no reference to magical divination in Stamford or Compo, but Mercy

Disborough's neighbors did use defensive magic to identify who was bewitching them and to inflict revenge. When Henry Grey's cow seemed strangely afflicted, he cut off part of the cow's ear and gave the animal a thrashing. The next day, Goody Disborough was confined to her bed with aches and pains. Goodman Grey concluded that this was a case of cause and effect: the injuries had been translated back onto Mercy Disborough as the afflicting witch. She was clearly to blame. He then described his experiment to the court as incriminating evidence.

New Englanders such as Henry Grey did not see anything wrong with using magic to defend themselves or to punish the wicked; only those who deployed their skills for malign ends were a social menace. From this perspective, witchcraft was the misuse of otherwise benign supernatural skills. But ministers saw things differently. They were horrified by the popularity of magical techniques, especially among devout settlers. They insisted that scripture gave no sanction for such experiments and that human beings could not wield supernatural forces. The Puritan clergy did not doubt that magic worked, but according to them it did so because the Devil intervened to assist whoever used it. Individuals might think that they were successfully harnessing occult powers, but in fact the Devil was doing it for them and so luring them into his service. Ministers denounced the use of magic to identify witches as "going to the Devil to find the Devil." All such experiments, regardless of whether the goal was benign or malevolent, were diabolical, their practitioners "beguiled by the serpent that lies in the grass unseen."[11]

Yet, in general, colonists who turned to magic do not seem to have given much thought to where such powers came from.

Ministers were deeply concerned with issues of causation and some of their congregants shared that concern, but other New Englanders were more concerned with results. Their attitude was pragmatic: tradition taught that such forces existed and that they could be useful. Some settlers may not have understood why magic was objectionable from a theological perspective; others may have understood quite well their ministers' objections, but quietly ignored official warnings or set aside their own misgivings for the simple reason that magic answered certain needs for knowledge and control that Puritan theology reserved only for God. When godly colonists turned to magic, they were not rejecting their religious faith so much as turning to whatever supernatural resource seemed helpful at a given moment. Mary Sibley, the Salem Village church member who asked Tituba to bake a urine-cake, was probably also praying to God for the child's deliverance from affliction. She may well have felt that her niece needed all the help she could get.

The belief that magic could be used for both good and evil purposes placed people like Tituba, known for their magical cunning, in an ambiguous and potentially perilous position. When New Englanders feared that they were bewitched, they often blamed men and women in their local communities who already had a reputation for occult skill: such individuals might be using their skills to harm as well as to help their neighbors. Tituba was one of the first to be accused in Salem Village. Healers could easily become the target of suspicion if their patients grew sicker instead of recovering. And anyone known for their magical expertise had reason to worry if they argued with a neighbor who then suffered a mysterious illness or mishap. Neighbors might conclude that they, their loved ones, or their possessions were bewitched. If they thought they had sufficient evidence to justify their claims in a court of law, the target of suspicion could well find herself on trial for her life.

WOMEN AS WITCHES

Women known for their magical skills were much more likely than men to be accused of witchcraft. The power wielded by cunning folk was potentially dangerous whether in the hands of a man or a woman, but it seemed especially threatening if possessed by a woman because it contradicted gender norms that placed women in subordinate positions. Neither belief in folk magic nor its practice were specific to women: men also resorted to and functioned as cunning folk. Yet suspicions that magical skill had been used for malicious ends were much more likely to be directed against female practitioners. Their prosecution testified not only to the ambiguous place that cunning folk occupied within New England communities but also to fear and suspicion of women in particular.

Witchcraft was perceived on both sides of the Atlantic as a primarily female phenomenon. Around four-fifths of those New Englanders tried for witchcraft were women. Roughly half of the men charged with this crime were married or otherwise close to accused women: they were, in other words, guilty by association.[12] Puritan ministers did not teach that women were by nature more evil than men, but they did see them as weaker and thus more susceptible to sinful impulses. Historian Elizabeth Reis has pointed out that "colonists shared with their English brethren the belief that women's bodies were physically weaker than men's" and that therefore "the Devil could more frequently and successfully gain access to and possess women's souls."[13] Ministers reminded New England congregations that it was Eve who first gave way to Satan and then seduced Adam, when she should have continued to serve his moral welfare in obedience to God; all women inherited that insidious blend of weakness and power from their mother Eve. Yet some women were much more likely to be accused of witchcraft than others. Throughout the seventeenth century, women became vulnerable to such allegations only if they were seen as having forsaken their prescribed place in a gendered hierarchy that Puritans held to be ordained by God.

Indeed, women who fulfilled their allotted roles as wives, mothers, household mistresses, and church members were respected and praised by their godly brethren as Handmaidens of the Lord. Puritan ministers insisted that women were not "a necessary evil" but instead "a necessary good," designed as a "sweet and intimate companion" for men.[14] That benign view of womankind contrasted sharply with entrenched stereotypes of women as morally untrustworthy. It was driven by an emphasis within the Protestant movement on the family as a primary agent of spiritual growth and social order. Like other English folk, Puritans worried about the disorder and godless behavior pervading their society. But, whereas most of their contemporaries favored the strengthening of civil and ecclesiastical authority to meet this challenge, Puritans advocated a more fundamental shift from external to internal discipline. Individuals, they proclaimed, should be trained to control themselves at an early age. This could be accomplished most effectively within the family household, as parents lovingly but firmly crushed the willful impulses of their children and taught them self-discipline.

That enterprise required a close and mutually supportive alliance between husband and wife. Though the husband as patriarch would have ultimate authority within the household, his wife must play a crucial role as "helpmeet" to him if their family was to fulfill its ordained purpose in fostering pious and well-ordered behavior. As historian Carol Karlsen has pointed out, Puritan thinkers needed to believe that women could play a constructive role within a godly commonwealth, not because they valued women in their own right but because they needed companions and helpmeets in the endeavor of raising self-disciplined and godly children. "There was no place in this vision," Karlsen writes, "for the belief that women were *incapable* of fulfilling such a role. Nor was there a place in the ideal Puritan society for women who refused to fill it."[15]

That caveat in Puritan gender ideology could prove fatal. Women whose circumstances or behavior seemed to disrupt social norms and hierarchies could easily lose their status as Handmaidens of the Lord and become branded as the Servants of Satan. Especially vulnerable were women who had passed menopause and thus no longer served the purpose of procreation, women who were widowed and so neither fulfilled the role of wife nor had a husband to protect them from malicious accusations, and women who had inherited or stood to inherit property in violation of expectations that wealth would be transmitted from man to man. Women who seemed unduly aggressive and contentious or who failed to display deference toward men in positions of authority—women, in other words, like Elizabeth Clawson and Mercy Disborough—were also more likely to be accused. Both Clawson and Disborough had husbands who were still alive, but they did fit the age profile of most accused witches: Goody Clawson was sixty-one and Goody Disborough was fifty-two. Both were also confident and determined, ready to express their opinions and to stand their ground when crossed. Such conduct seemed to many New Englanders utterly inappropriate in women.

The Protestant Reformation in general and Puritan culture in particular created an ambiguity in women's status that seems to have fostered anxiety about independent-minded women. The Protestant belief in a "priesthood of all believers," rejecting the Catholic emphasis on intercession by male priests, made women as well as men fully responsible for their own souls as they sought forgiveness for their sinfulness through direct engagement with God. Historian Christina Larner has suggested that the increase in witch accusations during the Reformation period may have functioned "as a rearguard action against the emergence of women as independent adults." After all, she notes, witchcraft "was only possible for women who had free will and responsibility attributed to them."[16]

Even as they stressed the important roles played by wives and mothers within the family household, Protestants reaffirmed patriarchal order. New Englanders sought to ensure a positive and respected place for women in godly society, yet lingering fear of "women-as-witches" complicated and compromised their celebration of women as "a necessary good." Behavior or circumstances that seemed disorderly could easily become identified as diabolical and associated with witchcraft: the Devil had, after all, led a rebellion against God's rule in heaven. Eve's legacy as a female prototype was double-edged: one the one hand, a beloved and successful helpmeet in the Garden of Eden; on the other, Satan's first human ally. Though worthy of honor as Adam's companion prior to their fall from grace, Eve's disobedience to God at the Devil's bidding made her the first witch.[17]

And what of Katherine Branch? Kate claimed at one point during her ordeal that the Devil had tried to recruit her as a witch. Once she became the center of attention in the household where she worked and indeed throughout Stamford, Kate assumed a prominence that was altogether anomalous for a young woman in New England society. She was also the object of much distrust. Given that witches were often described as eager to enlist new recruits, using physical pain and threats of various kinds as incentives to cooperate, there was a fine line between being assaulted by witches and becoming a witch suspect. Yet Kate herself was not accused of witchcraft. One of the afflicted girls in Salem did end up being accused, but most of the children and young women in seventeenth-century New England who claimed to be attacked by witches or possessed by the Devil managed to avoid such a fate. Those who appeared to be under assault by malign supernatural forces were generally treated as victims who deserved sympathy, even though their situation and behavior during those attacks often violated social norms; those who seemed voluntarily to embody evil were quite another matter.[18]

THE NEIGHBOR AS WITCH

When seventeenth-century New Englanders suspected that they were bewitched, whether by a woman or a man, the person they blamed was usually a close neighbor with whom they had a history of personal tension or conflict. Accuser and accused mostly lived within the same cluster of houses, often next-door or just across the street. In most cases the antagonism developed according to one of two scenarios. In some instances the accused witch had requested a loan or gift, perhaps of food or a household implement; the neighbor refused, which gave rise to anger and resentment. In others, an exchange of goods went awry as one neighbor accused another of deception or dishonesty. In the weeks, months, and even years that followed, the person who had turned down a neighbor's request for help or accused a neighbor of deceit blamed that same individual for later misfortunes. Abigail Wescot and Elizabeth Clawson had quarreled over the weight of some flax that Goody Clawson had provided; Henry Grey had accused Mercy Disborough's mother of lying about the weight of some apples and then accused Mercy herself of selling him a kettle that was supposedly new and yet turned out to be old and battered. Both Elizabeth Clawson and Mercy Disborough were infuriated by these claims. The assumption underlying most accusations of witchcraft was that a person who clearly felt mistreated turned to witchcraft as a form of revenge: the victim of witchcraft had failed to be a good neighbor, whether through lack of generosity or by questioning a neighbor's honesty, and so the alleged witch retaliated by becoming the ultimately nightmarish neighbor, wreaking havoc and destruction within her enemy's household.

Accusations of witchcraft were hardly a constant occurrence in early New England, yet many communities did have residents who were suspected of witchcraft. On over sixty occasions during the seventeenth century, excluding the witch hunt at Salem, such suspicions turned into formal charges of witchcraft. Most of these allegations originated in disputes between neighbors. This happened not because New Englanders were exceptionally vengeful or vicious, but because of an intersection between their social values and their supernatural beliefs. That social element, so crucial in witch accusations, was closely linked to the circumstances in which most premodern men and women lived.

Historian John Demos reminds us in his book *Entertaining Satan* that most New Englanders lived in tiny communities where the quality of life was "personal in the fullest sense."[19] Each resident not only knew everyone else in the town but also interacted with neighbors in many different roles and contexts. Most of us live in large towns or cities with populations in the tens of thousands and upward. Many of us have not met all the neighbors on our street or in our apartment complex, let alone those who live in other parts of the town or city. Different people fulfill distinct and isolated functions in our lives: when we go to the bank, a government office, or a shopping mall, the chances are that the official, cashier, or salesperson with whom we deal will be a stranger; even if we have dealt with the person before, it is unlikely that we know him or her in any other capacity. The experience of a New England settler could not have been more different. Demos invites us to envisage the following likely scenario:

> The brickmaker who rebuilds your chimney is also the constable who brings you a summons to court, an occupant of the next bench in the meetinghouse, the owner of a share adjacent to one of yours in the "upland" meadow, a rival for water-rights to the stream that flows behind that meadow, a fellow-member of the local "train

band" (i.e., militia), an occasional companion at the local "ordinary" (i.e., tavern), a creditor (from services performed for you the
previous summer but not as yet paid for), a potential customer for
wool from the sheep you have begun to raise, the father of a child
who is currently a bond-servant in your house, a colleague on a
town committee to repair and improve the public roadways . . .
And so on. Do the two of you enjoy your shared experiences? Not
necessarily. Do you know each other well? Most certainly.[20]

Personal interactions and influence were central to the experience of early New Englanders. It therefore made good sense to
account for misfortune or suffering in personal terms (just as it
should not surprise us that modern Americans inhabiting an often anonymous world, seemingly captive to faceless institutions,
should sometimes blame impersonal forces like "the federal
government" for their problems). Witchcraft explained personal
problems in terms of personal interactions. A particular neighbor had quarreled with you and was now taking revenge for a
perceived injury by bewitching you.

The tiny communities in which New Englanders settled were
clustered precariously on the margins of empire, separated from
each other by roads that were sometimes impassable and by no
means always safe. Neighbors knew that they depended on each
other for their survival. Townsfolk and villagers helped each
other to put up new buildings or harvest crops; they exchanged
food and simple products such as candles or soap in a local barter
economy; and they gave each other emotional support as they
navigated life's challenges and tragedies. The Puritan faith in
which most of the colonists believed (albeit to varying degrees)
taught that being a good neighbor had its spiritual as well as prac-

tical dimensions. Settlers must keep watch over each other, warn each other when they seemed to be in danger of giving way to sinful urges, and trust that others would keep an equally close eye on them.

John Winthrop, the first governor of Massachusetts, captured that spirit of mutual reliance in his famous lay sermon, "A Model of Christian Charity," delivered on board the *Arbella* in 1630 as the colonists approached Massachusetts Bay:

> We must be knit together in this work as one man. We must entertain each other in brotherly affection, we must be willing to abridge ourselves of our superfluities for the supply of others' necessities. We must uphold a familiar commerce together in all meekness, gentleness, patience, and liberality. We must delight in each other, make others' conditions our own, rejoice together, mourn together, labor and suffer together, always having before our eyes our commission and community in the work, our community as members of the same body. So shall we keep the unity of the spirit in the bond of peace.

These were stirring words, but easier to follow in theory than in practice. The Puritans' emphasis on community and mutual support meant that arguments between neighbors became not only irritating in their own right but also a betrayal of larger values on which their spiritual and practical welfare depended. It is, then, hardly surprising that such disputes gave rise to festering resentments.

In many instances there was no institutional outlet for the tensions and hostilities that resulted. If someone trespassed on a neighbor's property or assaulted another town resident, a law had been broken and the malefactor would be dealt with accordingly. But refusing to lend a neighbor food or a tool was not a crime and so the resulting animosity could not be expressed or mediated directly through civil or criminal proceedings. Witchcraft allegations provided an outlet for feelings of guilt or hostility rooted in confrontations between neighbors over issues of mutual support and responsibility. In one sense accusations of witchcraft performed a positive function in that they enabled men and women to express such feelings. Yet the atmosphere of suspicion, accusation, and recrimination that accompanied a trial could shred the social fabric; hostilities could linger for many years after the trial had run its course.

In England and Europe, historians have argued, conflicts between neighbors became particularly acute during the sixteenth and seventeenth centuries. The emergence of a market economy and increasing social mobility chipped away at time-honored values that centered on a local community's responsibility to care for its own; at the same time economic transformation swelled the ranks of the poverty-stricken who needed support from their neighbors. In time, new institutions like the workhouse would emerge to care for the needy, but meanwhile witchcraft accusations served as a double-edged response to unwelcome requests from neighbors in need. They defended traditional values by acknowledging that unneighborly behavior had negative consequences and yet legitimized new, less communitarian values by shifting attention away from the original unneighborly act to refocus on the anger of those who made unwelcome demands on their neighbors.[21]

The religious ideology to which New Englanders were exposed in sermons and other official pronouncements reaffirmed traditional values of neighborly support, yet the colonists themselves had left behind the communities in which they were raised and had to rely on a transatlantic commercial network for goods that they could not produce themselves. As they sought to reconstruct a sense of community in North America, sometimes settling in groups of families from the same town or county in England, they placed themselves under great pressure to abide by ideals that were perhaps unrealistic and that sometimes conflicted with other impulses. Under such circumstances tension and conflict became weighed down with guilt and resentment.[22]

Although most accusations of witchcraft originated in tensions between close neighbors, we should beware of concluding that New Englanders used such allegations as a cynical ploy to get rid of their enemies. Most of those who accused their neighbors of witchcraft believed quite sincerely that they were guilty as charged. Given the density of interpersonal contact in these tiny communities, it is hardly surprising that one neighbor's suspicions about another often spread from household to household in a ripple effect that encouraged other townsfolk to interpret their own misfortunes as the result of witchcraft. Allegations of witchcraft brought together three important components of premodern culture: the inability to explain or control illness and other forms of misfortune, a deeply embedded belief in supernatural forces that could be used to inflict harm, and the densely personal nature of human interactions. The mysterious and the supernatural converged with what John Demos refers to as "things most tangible and personal." Along "the seam of their convergence" emerged accusations of witchcraft.[23]

Witch Trials in Seventeenth-Century New England

Once New Englanders became convinced that a particular individual had bewitched them, they had the right to lodge a formal complaint and so initiate a criminal prosecution. In England and its New England colonies, allegations of witchcraft were handled by secular courts, not the ecclesiastical courts of inquisition that conducted witch trials in some European countries. The wording of New England's laws against witchcraft was inspired by religious doctrine and the penalty of death was justified by reference to scripture. But the trial process itself was in the hands of secular officials.

New England's legal system was rigorous and cautious in its handling of capital cases. Convincing oneself and one's neighbors of an individual's guilt was not the same as convincing a court. Of the sixty-one known prosecutions for witchcraft in seventeenth-century New England, excluding the Salem witch hunt, sixteen at most (perhaps only fourteen) resulted in conviction and execution, a rate of just over one-quarter (26.2 percent). Four of the accused individuals confessed, which made the court's job much easier. If those cases are omitted, the conviction rate falls to just under one-fifth (19.7 percent).[24]

Puritan theology depicted witches as heretical servants of the Devil. The legal code also defined witchcraft in theological terms, demanding proof of diabolical allegiance. Yet ordinary men and women were more inclined to think about witchcraft as a practical problem; they were interested less in causation than they were in results. They believed that witchcraft was at work in their communities; they wanted to know who the witch was; and they wanted her punished. Excluding the Salem witch hunt, which produced many testimonies to the Devil's involvement, depositions in most witch cases reflected that practical preoccupation and rarely made any mention of the Devil. That disjunction between legal requirements and popular testimony led to acquittal in most cases. We might wonder why witnesses did not adapt their testimony to fit legal requirements. That they did not do so suggests that ordinary colonists focused quite doggedly on practical issues when thinking about witchcraft and also that at least some people were much less thoroughly schooled in official ideology than our stereotypes of early New Englanders would suggest.[25]

The evidence given against New England's accused witches generally fell into one of four categories. Most frequently, witnesses described quarrels followed by misfortune or illness, presumably brought on by witchcraft. Second, witnesses claimed that the accused had a reputation for skill as a fortune teller or healer; this established that the accused had occult powers which, it was implied, had also been deployed for malign purposes. Third, witnesses described having used defensive and retaliatory techniques such as Henry Grey inflicted on his heifer; they reported the results of such experiments to the court as incriminating testimony. And finally, neighbors of the accused would describe generally suspicious behavior, such as extraordinary and perhaps superhuman strength.

Like the depositions given at the trials of Elizabeth Clawson and Mercy Disborough, most testimony presented at witch trials in New England proved unconvincing from the perspective of legal and religous experts. As we have seen, magistrates and learned ministers dismissed testimony relating "strange accidents" following quarrels as "slender and uncertain grounds" for conviction. Clergymen denounced defensive magic as "going to the Devil to find the Devil" and warned that Satan was a malicious liar, which hardly encouraged magistrates to convict based on depositions that described such experiments.[26] Judges were occasionally willing to conclude that divination or other magical practices proved collusion between the accused witch and the Devil (ministers did, after all, condemn such techniques as diabolical); but even here magistrates were loathe to convict unless the incriminating testimony made explicit mention of the Devil.

New England witch trials resulted in fewer convictions than did their counterparts across the Atlantic. English statutes enacted against witchcraft in 1542 and 1563 had defined the crime as a hostile act rather than as heresy, so that popular preoccupation with practical harm was more compatible with legal requirements. Laws in European countries generally defined witchcraft as a diabolical heresy, but there the courts often used torture to extract the kinds of evidence that would justify conviction. English law forbade the use of torture during judicial interrogation and the New England authorities operated under English jurisdiction. The only occasion on which New England courts gathered extensive evidence of diabolical allegiance was the Salem witch hunt, which was also the one occasion on which the authorities made illegal use of physical torture and extreme psychological pressure to extract a large number of confessions.

New England magistrates were willing to convict and execute accused witches. But as in the Puritans' handling of prosecutions for other capital crimes, the courts refused to convict unless the evidence satisfied rigorous standards of proof: this meant either a voluntary confession, or at least two independent witnesses to an incident demonstrating the individual's guilt. It was difficult enough to secure two witnesses for other offenses that carried the death penalty, such as adultery and rape.[27] But the challenge was compounded when dealing with an invisible crime that involved collusion with supernatural agents. Witnesses assumed that their personal experiences and impressions would be treated as hard evidence, but judges were interested only in evidence that established diabolical involvement and even then worried about its reliability. Accusers risked their lives in speaking out against a witch, but magistrates also took a risk if they approved the conviction of a witch suspect on the basis of dubious evidence—they might very well be executing an innocent person. Only in a quarter of cases did New England magistrates find the evidence sufficient to justify conviction.

The neighbors and enemies of accused witches who had given what they considered to be damning testimony were often infuriated by the reluctance of magistrates to treat their depositions as legally compelling. From the perspective of many modern Americans, the execution of any person accused of witchcraft seems tragic and unjust. But in the minds of men and women who did not doubt witchcraft's malevolent power, the acquittal and release of witch suspects was the gross miscarriage of justice. Neighbors sometimes refused to accept an acquittal, conferred with each other, gathered new evidence against the suspect, and then renewed legal charges. Three New Englanders were each prosecuted for witchcraft on three separate occasions; another five appeared in court twice on charges of witchcraft. All of these cases resulted in acquittal.[28] As the difficulty of securing a legal conviction for witchcraft became increasingly apparent, New Englanders became less inclined to initiate legal prosecutions against suspected witches. Nor were officials eager to take on such cases. There were nineteen witch trials in New England during the 1660s, but only six during the 1670s and eight during the 1680s. Elizabeth Clawson and Mercy Disborough were the first residents of Connecticut to stand trial for that crime in over twenty years.

ESCAPING SALEM

The dramatic fall in the number of prosecutions for witchcraft during the 1670s and 1680s was not due to any decline in fear of witches. The persistence of that fear became only too clear in 1692, when official encouragement of witch accusations in and around Salem Village resulted in over one hundred and fifty arrests and nineteen executions. We know that news of events in Massachusetts had reached Connecticut by the time townsfolk and villagers came forward to corroborate Katherine Branch's claim that Goody Clawson and Goody Disborough were witches. The deluge of accusations in Massachusetts and the willingness of officials there to take such allegations seriously doubtless encouraged the smaller but still potentially deadly witch hunt in Fairfield County, Connecticut. Settlers who had kept silent for years about their suspicions against Elizabeth Clawson and Mercy Disborough now felt that surely the courts would have to listen and act. They were to be sorely disappointed.

The witch hunt that took place in Connecticut that year provides a useful corrective to the Salem story. Indeed, the hysteria that erupted in Salem Village has long distorted our perception of early New England.[29] The scale and intensity of that witch hunt was due in large part to its immediate context, a series of recent crises in the region that included a renewal of Indian attacks in northern New England and increased activity by dissenters such as Anglicans and Quakers. These disturbances had fostered intense anxiety among the residents of Massachusetts, who described the physical and spiritual assaults of those years in much the same language that they used to describe witchcraft: as alien, malign, and invasive. Many believed that Indians worshiped the Devil and that Quakers were possessed by Satan. It is no coincidence that Andover, which in 1692 produced more accusations of witchcraft than Salem Village itself, was the first nonfrontier community to have townsmen killed by Indians when a new round of Anglo–Indian hostilities began at the end of the 1680s. Nor was it coincidental that next to Salem Village was the largest concentration of Quaker households in the county. To the colonists, the outbreak of witchcraft in Salem Village was the latest in a series of terrifying demonic assaults that threatened to overwhelm them.

The magistrates charged with handling the resulting panic encouraged accusations and proceeded to convict on the basis of evidence that was by normal legal standards deeply problematic. They did so with the approval of the royal governor and other prominent citizens. Historian Mary Beth Norton has suggested that the support given by Massachusetts leaders to the special court was due in no small part to their own lack of success in repelling Indian attacks: rooting out those responsible for invisible assaults on the colony would deflect attention away from and lessen their own sense of guilt for failing to deal more effectively with more visible enemies. The result was by far the largest and deadliest witch hunt in seventeenth-century New England.[30]

The accusations and legal proceedings in Connecticut that year were much more typical of other witch trials in New England. The cast of characters involved in the Salem drama can so easily become caricatured as credulous and even hysterical, but townsfolk in Stamford were for the most part more restrained and skeptical, doing their best to unravel the mystery surrounding Katherine Branch's fits, conducting careful experiments to confirm or refute their suspicions, conferring with each other to compare stories and weigh the evidence. Some residents were unwilling to believe the allegations against Elizabeth Clawson and Mercy Disborough, not because they doubted the reality of witchcraft but because they questioned whether these particular women were witches. The magistrates were also remarkably cautious: while they had no desire to dismiss or belittle the fears of those who believed that Goody Clawson and Goody Disborough were bewitching their neighbors, they were also determined to meet their own rigorous standards of proof. At least some of those involved in Connecticut's witch hunt viewed their local crisis in the context of recent events in Salem. The committee that reprieved Mercy Disborough warned explicitly against repeating the errors of judgment that had already led to tragedy in Massachusetts. Like most modern readers, their perspective on what was happening in Connecticut was shaped partly by their knowledge of the infamous trials further north.

Perhaps one of the most striking similarities between these two witch hunts was that both ended in the release of witch suspects whom significant numbers of people believed to be guilty. Following the suspension of legal proceedings in Salem—in large part because of mounting controversy over the evidence being used to convict defendants—those not yet tried and convicted were released to rejoin their families and resume, as best they could, their normal lives. Nineteen people had been convicted and hanged; one man was crushed to death by stones loaded on his chest because he would not enter a plea of "innocent" or "guilty"; several other individuals died in prison. But over a hundred imprisoned suspects now went free. In Connecticut no executions took place as a result of the special court's deliberations, though Mercy Disborough came very close to losing her life.

Popular disillusionment and official embarrassment following the debacle at Salem and legal wrangles in Connecticut combined to bring about an end to witch trials in New England. By the early eighteenth century a degree of skepticism about certain kinds of allegedly supernatural phenomena began to take hold among those Americans who embraced Enlightenment ideas. But belief in a world of wonders and occult afflictions proved resilient among other Americans. People continued to use defensive magic against witchcraft throughout the eighteenth century. In July 1787, as delegates met in Philadelphia to draft the federal constitution, a woman sustained fatal injuries inflicted by a mob in the city streets because they believed that she was a witch.[31]

Today we neither hang nor assault suspected witches. But we have experienced our own share of witch hunts in the form of campaigns against people accused of unpopular or unconventional views, usually with little evidence. When Arthur Miller wrote his play *The Crucible*, first performed in 1953 during Senator Joseph McCarthy's campaign to root out communist "subversives" and spies, Miller sought to remind us that the mobilization of fear, suspicion, and malice can still have devastating results. The impulse to find a scapegoat in times of trouble and to demonize those whom we dislike and fear remains very much alive. Jews and other ethnoreligious groups, communists and capitalists, feminists and homosexuals, liberals and conservatives, religious fundamentalists—each group has figured in the minds of its enemies as an evil and alien force that threatens to corrode and destroy. A periodic need for witch hunts would appear to be one

It was in response to a political "witch hunt" in the early 1950s, target-ing people suspected of Communist sympathies and led by Senator Joseph McCarthy, that Arthur Miller wrote The Crucible, *a powerful and mov-ing dramatization of the tragic events that took place in Salem. Miller was himself summoned before the Un-American Activities Committee.* (SOURCE: REPRODUCED BY PERMISSION OF THE LIBRARY OF CONGRESS.)

of the more resilient as well as one of the least admirable human instincts.

Nor has a fear of power in the hands of women disappeared along with witch trials. Women who assume positions of visible authority still arouse hostility on both sides of the Atlantic. In the 1980s, the organizers of a Labour Party rally in England to protest rising unemployment under Margaret Thatcher's government planned to use "Ditch the Witch" as their slogan until someone protested that this was sexist—they then relented and used "Ditch the Bitch" instead.[32] Equally venomous attacks on Hilary Rodham Clinton during her husband's term of office as President of the United States in the 1990s expressed an intense, fearful response on the part of some Americans to the First Lady's personality and behavior, which challenged still powerful precepts about a woman's role in American society.

None of the impulses that drive witch hunts (seventeenth-century or modern) are necessarily cynical or insincere—they reflect genuine fears as well as the impulse to lash out when frightened or thwarted. But theologians in early New England recommended a counterbalance to that impulse that remains applicable today: they argued that any legitimate response to adversity must involve self-scrutiny and the acknowledgment that we are sometimes at least partly responsible for our own misfortunes. Few of us today would wish to identify too closely with the Puritan tendency to extreme self-censure, yet accepting the possibility that the blame for one's problems might not always lie entirely with others strikes me as morally necessary and constructive. Yet a voyage into one's own moral interior can be alarming and unwelcome. That people chose then and still choose now to demonize others instead of recognizing their own share of human frailty is one of our most persistent tragedies.

NOTES

1. Gershom Bulkeley to Joseph Bulkeley, 3 June 1696, in Donald Lines Jacobus, ed., *History and Genealogy of the Families of Old Fairfield*, 2 vols. (1930–32; Baltimore: Genealogical Publishing Co., 1976), 2:300–302.

2. Ibid., 1:187.

3. Ibid. 1:148–49; Jeanne Majdaleny, *The Early Settlement of Stamford, 1641–1700* (Bowie, Md.: Heritage Books, 1990), 154–55.

4. See Jon Butler, *The Huguenots in America: A Refugee People in New World Society* (Cambridge, Mass.: Harvard University Press, 1983).

5. Jacobus, *History and Genealogy*, 1:661–62.

6. Keith Thomas, *Religion and the Decline of Magic* (New York: Scribners, 1971), 5.

7. Ibid., 9.

8. David D. Hall, *Worlds of Wonder, Days of Judgment: Popular Religious Belief in Early New England* (New York: Knopf, 1989), 11, 71.

9. John Dane, "A Declaration of Remarkable Providences in the Course of My Life," in *Remarkable Providences: Readings on Early American History*, ed. John Demos (Boston: Northeastern University Press, 1991), 63.

10. For a detailed examination of magical lore and practice, see Richard Godbeer, *The Devil's Dominion: Magic and Religion in Early New England* (New York: Cambridge University Press, 1992), esp. Chap. 1. For more on Tituba see Elaine G. Breslaw, *Tituba, Reluctant Witch of Salem: Devilish Indians and Puritan Fantasies* (New York: New York University Press, 1996).

11. John Hale, *A Modest Enquiry into the Nature of Witchcraft* (Boston, 1702), 21, 248–49. For discussion of clerical opposition to magic, see Godbeer, *The Devil's Dominion*, Chap. 2.

12. Carol Karlsen, *The Devil in the Shape of a Woman: Witchcraft in Colonial New England* (New York: Norton, 1987), 47–48. For a recent study of men accused as witches in their own right, see Lara Apps and Andrew Gow, *Male Witches in Early Modern Europe* (Manchester, U.K.: Manches-

ter University Press, 2003). Contrary to conventional wisdom, Apps and Gow argue that in some parts of Europe more men than women were accused of witchcraft.

13. Elizabeth Reis, *Damned Women: Sinners and Witches in Puritan New England* (Ithaca, N.Y.: Cornell University Press, 1997), 108, 110.

14. John Cotton, *A Meet Help* (Boston, 1699), 14, 21.

15. Karlsen, *The Devil in the Shape of a Woman*, 165.

16. Christina Larner, *Enemies of God: The Witch-Hunt in Scotland* (Baltimore: Johns Hopkins University Press, 1981), 101–2.

17. Karlsen discusses the demographic, economic, and temperamental characteristics of accused witches in *The Devil in the Shape of a Woman*, Chapters 2–4.

18. Children and young women who claimed to be possessed often engaged in illicit behavior—running amok, blaspheming, insulting authority figures, and disobeying parents or masters—without having to take the blame for their actions. After all, it was the witch or Devil that made them do it. Carol Karlsen argues that possession enabled powerless individuals to express discontent and rebel against those with authority in a context that would position them as victims: they could project their own illicit feelings onto the witch or Devil within. See Karlsen, *The Devil in the Shape of a Woman*, Chap. 7.

19. John Putnam Demos, *Entertaining Satan: Witchcraft and the Culture of Early New England* (New York: Oxford University Press, 1982), 312.

20. Ibid., 311–12.

21. See Alan Macfarlane, *Witchcraft in Tudor and Stuart England* (London: Routledge and Kegan Paul, 1970); Keith Thomas, "Anthropology and the Study of English Witchcraft," in *Witchcraft Confessions and Accusations*, ed. Mary Douglas (London: Tavistock Publications, 1970); and Max Marwick, "Witchcraft as a Social Stress-Gauge," in *Witchcraft and Sorcery: Selected Readings*, ed. Max Marwick (Harmondsworth, U.K.: Penguin, 1970).

22. That tension between the values of moral community and individual self-interest was at least partly responsible for the 1692 outbreak of witch accusations in Salem Village. Paul Boyer and Stephen Nissenbaum

have argued that factional conflicts within the village help to explain who accused whom that year and that those divisions were rooted in disputes over economic welfare and cultural values. See Paul Boyer and Stephen Nissenbaum, *Salem Possessed: The Social Origins of Witchcraft* (Cambridge, Mass.: Harvard University Press, 1974).

23. Demos, *Entertaining Satan*, 312.

24. Godbeer, *The Devil's Dominion*, 158.

25. Ibid., Chap. 5.

26. Hale, *A Modest Enquiry*, 21.

27. Richard Godbeer, *Sexual Revolution in Early America* (Baltimore: Johns Hopkins University Press, 2002), 102–4.

28. Godbeer, *The Devil's Dominion*, 172–73.

29. The volume of literature on Salem is immense. For a useful sampling, see Marc Mappen, ed., *Witches and Historians: Interpretations of Salem* (Malabar, Fla.: Krieger Publishing Company, 1996), and also Elaine G. Breslaw, ed., *Witches of the Atlantic World: A Historical Reader and Primary Sourcebook* (New York: New York University Press, 2000). Recent books on the subject include Bernard Rosenthal, *Salem Story: Reading the Witch Trials of 1692* (New York: Cambridge University Press, 1993); Frances Hill, *A Delusion of Satan: The Full Story of the Salem Witch Trials* (New York: Doubleday, 1995); Peter Hoffer, *The Devil's Disciples: Makers of the Salem Witchcraft Trials* (Baltimore: Johns Hopkins University Press, 1996); Bryan F. Le Beau, *The Story of the Salem Witch Trials* (Upper Saddle River, N.J.: Prentice Hall, 1998); and Mary Beth Norton, *In the Devil's Snare: The Salem Witchcraft Crisis of 1692* (New York: Knopf, 2002).

30. Norton, *In the Devil's Snare*, esp. 299–300.

31. For discussion of continued belief in witchcraft see Godbeer, *The Devil's Dominion*, 223–33.

32. Christina Larner, *Witchcraft and Religion: The Politics of Popular Belief* (Oxford, U.K.: Basil Blackwell, 1984), 84.

SELECT BIBLIOGRAPHY

A. THE CONNECTICUT WITCH HUNT OF 1692

Almost all of the documents surviving from the trials are to be found in the Wyllys Papers at the John Hay Library, Brown University, and the Samuel Wyllys Papers at the Connecticut State Library. The petition of 4 June 1692 supporting Elizabeth Clawson is owned by the Stamford Historical Society. Most of these documents have recently been published in David D. Hall, ed., *Witch-Hunting in Seventeenth-Century New England: A Documentary History, 1638–1693*, 2nd ed., Boston: Northeastern University Press, 1999, 315–54.

Historical Accounts of the Witch Hunt:

Marcus, Ronald. *"Elizabeth Clawson . . . Thou Deservest to Dye": An Account of the Trial in 1692 of a Woman from Stamford, Connecticut, Who Was Accused of Being a Witch*. Stamford, Conn.: Stamford Historical Society, 1976.

Taylor, John M. *The Witchcraft Delusion in Colonial Connecticut, 1647–1697*. New York: Grafton Press, 1908.

Tomlinson, Richard G. *Witchcraft Trials of Connecticut: The First Comprehensive, Documented History of Witchcraft Trials in Colonial Connecticut*. Hartford, Conn.: Connecticut Research, Inc., 1978.

Local Histories

Feinstein, Estelle S. *Stamford from Puritan to Patriot: The Shaping of a Connecticut Community, 1641–1774*. Stamford, Conn.: Stamford Bicentennial Corporation, 1976.

Huntington, Elijah B. *History of Stamford, Connecticut*. Stamford, Conn.: William Gillespie & Co., 1868.

Jacobus, Donald Lines. *History and Genealogy of the Families of Old Fairfield*, 2 vols. Fairfield, Conn., 1930–32.

McLean, Louise H. "The Sellecks of Early Stamford." *Darien Historical Society Annual* 1, no. 7 (March 1961): 3–9.

Majdalany, Jeanne. *The Early Settlement of Stamford, Connecticut, 1641–1700*. Bowie, Md.: Heritage Books, 1990.

B. WITCHCRAFT IN SEVENTEENTH-CENTURY NEW ENGLAND

Boyer, Paul and Stephen Nissenbaum. *Salem Possessed: The Social Origins of Witchcraft*. Cambridge, Mass.: Harvard University Press, 1974.

Breslaw, Elaine G. *Tituba, Reluctant Witch of Salem: Devilish Indians and Puritan Fantasies*. New York: New York University Press, 1996.

Demos, John Putnam. *Entertaining Satan: Witchcraft and the Culture of Early New England*. New York: Oxford University Press, 1982.

Godbeer, Richard. *The Devil's Dominion: Magic and Religion in Early New England*. New York: Cambridge University Press, 1992.

Godbeer, Richard. "Chaste and Unchaste Covenants: Witchcraft and Sex in Early Modern Culture." In *Wonders of the Invisible World, 1600–1900*, ed. Peter Benes. Boston: Boston University Press, 1995.

Hall, David D. *Worlds of Wonder, Days of Judgment: Popular Religious Belief in Early New England*. New York: Knopf, 1989.

Hall, David D. "Middle Ground on the Witch-Hunting Debate." *Reviews in American History* 26 (1998): 345–52.

Hansen, Chadwick. *Witchcraft at Salem*. New York: Braziller, 1969.

Harley, David. "Explaining Salem: Calvinist Psychology and the Diagnosis of Possession." *American Historical Review* 101 (1996): 307–30.

Hoffer, Peter Charles. *The Devil's Disciples: Makers of the Salem Witchcraft Trials*. Baltimore: Johns Hopkins University Press, 1996.

Kamensky, Jane. *Governing the Tongue: The Politics of Speech in Early New England*. New York: Oxford University Press, 1997.

Karlsen, Carol. *The Devil in the Shape of a Woman: Witchcraft in Colonial New England*. New York: Norton, 1987.

Norton, Mary Beth. *In the Devil's Snare: The Salem Witchcraft Crisis of 1692*. New York: Knopf, 2002.

Reis, Elizabeth. *Damned Women: Sinners and Witches in Puritan New England*. Ithaca, N.Y.: Cornell University Press, 1997.

Rosenthal, Bernard. *Salem Story: Reading the Witch Trials of 1692*. New York: Cambridge University Press, 1993.

Upham, Charles W. *Salem Witchcraft*. Boston: Wiggin and Lunt, 1867.

Weisman, Richard. *Witchcraft, Magic, and Religion in Seventeenth-Century Massachusetts*. Amherst: University of Massachusetts Press, 1984.

C. Witchcraft in Early Modern England and Europe

Ankerloo, Bengt, and Gustav Henningsen, eds. *Early Modern European Witchcraft: Centres and Peripheries*. Oxford, U.K.: Oxford University Press, 1990.

Apps, Lara, and Andrew Gow. *Male Witches in Early Modern Europe*. Manchester, U.K.: Manchester University Press, 2003.

Barstow, Anne L. *Witchcraze: A New History of the European Witch Hunts*. San Francisco: Harper, 1994.

Clark, Stuart. *Thinking With Demons: The Idea of Witchcraft in Early Modern Europe*. New York: Oxford University Press, 1997.

Clark, Stuart, ed. *Languages of Witchcraft: Narrative, Ideology, and Meaning in Early Modern Culture*. New York: St. Martin's Press, 2001.

Larner, Christina. *Enemies of God: The Witch-Hunt in Scotland*. Baltimore: Johns Hopkins University Press, 1981.

Larner, Christina. *Witchcraft and Religion: The Politics of Popular Belief*. Oxford, U.K.: Basil Blackwell, 1984.

Levack, Brian P. *The Witch-Hunt in Early Modern Europe*, 2nd ed. New York: Longman, 1995.

Macfarlane, Alan. *Witchcraft in Tudor and Stuart England*. London: Routledge and Kegan Paul, 1970.

Thomas, Keith. *Religion and the Decline of Magic*. New York: Scribners, 1971.